Gene Baer's

WILD & WONDERFUL ART LESSONS

Gene Baer's
WILD &
WONDERFUL
ART LESSONS

Parker Publishing Company, Inc. —————— West Nyack, New York

©1983 by

PARKER PUBLISHING COMPANY, INC.

West Nyack, N.Y.

10 9

Library of Congress Cataloging in Publication Data

Baer, Gene,
  Gene Baer's Wild & wonderful art lessons,

  Includes index.
  1. Art—Study and teaching (Elementary)—United
States. I. Title. II. Title: Gene Baer's Wild and
wonderful art lessons. III. Title: Wild & wonderful
art lessons. IV. Title: Wild and wonderful art lessons.
N362.B35   1983   372.5'044   83-8093

ISBN 0-13-347567-0

Printed in the United States of America

To Jackie with love

ABOUT THE AUTHOR

Gene Baer is the K-8 Art Specialist for the Town of Tisbury, Martha's Vineyard, Massachusetts. He began teaching after a successful career in illustration, beginning as an Army artist and as a technical illustrator for industry. He has done extensive free-lance commercial art and has sold cartoons to dozens of national publications.

Mr. Baer is also the author of two other practical resources for inservice classroom teachers and art specialists, *Paste, Pencils, Scissors and Crayons* (1979) and *Imaginative Art Lessons for Kids & Their Teachers* (1982), both published by Parker Publishing Company. The former was called by the publisher of *Art Education Digest* "the very best book for teachers I have ever seen."

A WORD FROM THE AUTHOR

Of all the unsung art forms, none rates higher in my mind than the well-crafted lesson plan. This book is the third in an ongoing series of art activity books that I am writing for Parker Publishing Company, and while each of these books is quite different from the others, all are filled with well-tested art lesson plans that are as fresh and entertaining as they are instructive.

Like you, I am a teacher. I work tight schedules in crowded classrooms that abound with large numbers of healthy, active, and demanding children. *Here* the most successful art lessons are always those that are easy to prepare, fun to present, and highly entertaining to do. A good lesson smiles!

The fun-filled lessons that you will find in this book are primarily of my own invention, and all clearly reflect my long and extensive classroom experience. Polished and buffed to a high degree of perfection by the rough-and-tumble action of large groups of children, every lesson is thoroughly child-tested and ready for immediate presentation. Not only are these lessons fun to do and easy to present, but all are intellectually exciting, thought-provoking, and instructive. Most of these lessons can be completed in a single session, and few need more than an additional period for finishing.

As to cost, since this is a budget-minded book, very few if any of the lessons included here call for supplies or materials that are not found in most elementary classrooms. If you have access to paper, paste (or glue), pencils, scissors, stapler, and crayons, you have all the material you need for the vast majority of these lessons, and those that call for additional materials do so sparingly and with a protective eye on your classroom budget.

In planning my lessons I always try to use the most efficient means at my disposal. Certain paper sizes, for example, are more economical than others, for they leave usable remainders. A 12" × 18" sheet of construction paper subdivides naturally into 6 × 18s, 9 × 12s, 6 × 9s, 4½ × 12s, 4½ × 6s, 3 × 4½s, 2¼ × 3s, etc. These dimensions are therefore among the fractional sizes most often called for in this book: a practice that leaves you with easy-to-stack, easy-to-use leftovers!

Since different catalog and supply houses often use different terminologies for identical or near-identical items, this fact of life always makes for some difficulty in writing a "needs list" that can be readily understood by others. For this reason I have tried to keep the terms used in my needs lists as generic as possible:

> By *drawing paper* I mean any kind of white or off-white "art" paper of approximately the same weight as standard construction paper.
>
> By *practice paper* I mean any kind of cheap newsprint (sometimes referred to by teachers as "math" paper) or even mimeo or duplicating papers. (These last two are more expensive, but they make excellent art materials and are always a great favorite with kids!)
>
> By *pattern-weight paperboard* I mean any kind of sturdy, lightweight paper stock (like *tagboard*) that has more substance than paper but less bulk than, say, poster or mat board.

Furthermore, through the years I have learned to make extensive use of certain concepts, shortcuts, and working procedures for which, to my knowledge, there are no verbal equivalents. Terms like *Sailboat Fold, Quarterbacking, Measuring Strips*, etc., are terms of my own invention, and while I apologize for their down-home ring, they are old friends that have served me well. To communicate this kind of hard-earned information effectively without a great deal of unnecessary duplication of instructional material, I have found it convenient to store most of this information in illustrated glossary form. (See pages 208-214.)

While some knowledge of art is always helpful to a teacher, there is nothing in this book that demands prior knowledge or special abilities. To assure the greatest possible clarity of communication, everything is written in clear, easy-to-follow procedural steps carefully keyed to hundreds of illustrations and diagrams. If there is any way to improve this book—I confess I don't know what it is!

Since each of the sections in this book is more or less self-sufficient, feel free simply to select a section at random and begin. After you have begun, don't be afraid to experiment or to follow intuitive hunches.

Have fun!

CONTENTS

In this edition of "W&W" I have added estimates as to the amount of time that should be scheduled for each activity. But a word of warning: If your experiences with these lessons parallel mine, you may discover that just when the estimated class time is coming to an end—a second wave of excitement may have already begun!

G.B

JUST
FOR
FUN

If a classroom activity can in some way provoke a sense of wonder in a child, that activity is by definition an educational triumph. And for most of us—*that's* what makes teaching fun!

Lesson 1   Decoration Birds

In one form or another I have given this lesson dozens of times, and it has always been one of the best. Now it's *yours*—enjoy it!

YOU NEED*

> practice paper
> 12″ × 18″ drawing paper
> pencils and crayons

Figure 1-1A

---

*For an attractive alternative to this needs list, add white chalk and substitute pastel-colored construction paper for the regular drawing paper.

TO PRESENT:

1. Explain to your kids that the subject for today's lesson is not *real* birds but make-believe ones, and that make-believe birds can be drawn in any way in which one wants to draw them.

Furthermore, explain to your kids that for today's purposes their make-believe birds should be drawn with very simple shapes, perhaps something like the ones shown here in Figures 1-1B, 1-1C, 1-1D, 1-1E.

2. Once your kids try out a few bird shapes on their practice paper, tell them to lightly pencil in the outline (only) of one large bird on their 12″ × 18″ pastel-colored paper.

3. Then, once their birds are drawn, have your kids divide up the surface of the birds with stripes. Two kinds of stripes can be suggested here: flat and form-fitting. (See Figures 1-1F and 1-1G.)

Figure 1-1B

Figure 1-1C

Figure 1-1D

Figure 1-1E

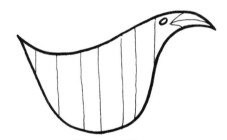

Figure 1-1F

Figure 1-1G

4. And finally, have your kids use their crayons to decorate this bird with colorful repeat patterns as suggested in Figure 1-1A.

Lesson 2   Scissor Birds

The emotional impact of a lesson cannot be easily predicted. I have spent long hours devising lesson plans that have flopped, and I have also invented spur-of-the-moment lessons that were fantastically successful. Here, for example, is a simple starter lesson that—for some reason or another—your kids will remember for years to come. Why this lesson should receive such an ovation, I don't know. But it does.!

YOU NEED:

12 " × 18 " drawing paper

practice paper

pencils, scissors, and crayons

Figure 1-2A

TO PRESENT:

1. In order to succeed in this lesson the child must be able to trace a pair of scissors. For little kids this is not an easy

task. Your best bet here is to encourage them to help each other; one holds, the other traces. Have them practice tracing the scissors in the two positions indicated in Figures 1-2B and 1-2C.

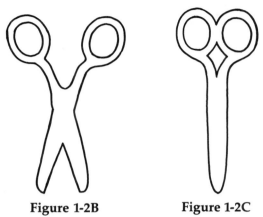

Figure 1-2B   **Figure 1-2C**

2.   Once your kids have traced a couple of different positions, invite them to turn these tracings into "scissor birds" as shown in Figures 1-2D and 1-2E.

3.   Then pass out the 12" × 18" drawing paper and let them go to work arranging the birds into a theme of their own choice! (See Figure 1-2A.)

Figure 1-2D   **Figure 1-2E**

Lesson 3   Spring Hoop Snakes

Kids love to make paper chains, but the only time they ever get to make them is at Christmas time. The *Spring Hoop Snake* should change all that!

YOU NEED:

construction paper in the following colors and sizes:
  9″ × 12″ and (two) 6″ × 9″ yellow-green (or any other appropriate snake color)
  ¼″ × 9″ red
  small scraps of black and white
9″ × 12″ pattern-weight paperboard
stapler
paste, pencils, scissors, and crayons

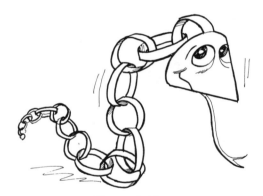

Figure 1-3A

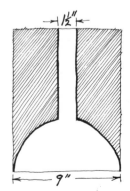

Figure 1-3B

PREPARATIONS:

Using the 9″ × 12″ pattern-weight paperboard, prepare a pattern that looks something like the one illustrated in Figure 1-3B. Cut away the shaded areas.

TO PRESENT:

1.   Have your kids trace the tag pattern onto the 9″ × 12″ yellow-green, and then cut it out.

2. *Your* job is to staple the long, handle-like part to the semicircular part as shown in Figure 1-3C. Circlecone* and staple. (See Figure 1-3D.)

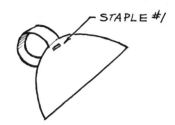

Figure 1-3C

Figure 1-3D

3. The white paper is for making eyes; the black paper, for the pupils.

4. Using the point of the scissors, poke a hole for the mouth that is large enough to receive one end of the red "tongue." Paste the root of the tongue to the inside of the snake's head.

5. As for the rest of the body—that's easy! The 6" × 9" paper is cut up into 6" strips and the strips are pasted chain-style to form the snake's body!

Lesson 4   On-Off Flashlight Pictures

Kids like any kind of a lesson in which lights can be turned on and off. And what lends itself better to this kind of treatment than a flashlight picture!

---

*See Glossary.

YOU NEED:

9″ × 12″ light blue construction paper

9″ × 12″ manila drawing paper

paste, pencils, scissors, and crayons

Figure 1-4A

TO PRESENT:

1.   Using their 9″ × 12″ light blue construction paper in a horizontal position, have your kids draw some kind of an after dark flashlight scene in which the figure holding the flashlight is positioned to one side of the paper and is directing the beam toward the other side of the paper. (See Figure 1-4B.)

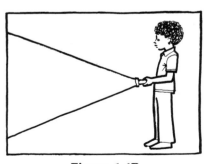

Figure 1-4B

Possible picture ideas might include: looking for a lost toy, playing flashlight tag, a camping trip, going down a dark street, etc. (See Figure 1-4C.)

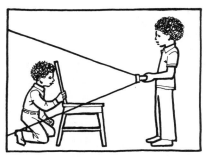

Figure 1-4C

2.   Once this picture has been completed, invite your kids to use their scissors to cut out the "light." Once this is done, have them paste the light blue paper to the manila and draw in the missing parts in the newly illuminated section as suggested in Figure 1-4A.

3.   Oh yes—one final suggestion. No sooner will your kids complete their pictures than someone will discover that the cut-away piece can be put to good use—restore it and the flashlight goes off, take it away and the light goes on again!

Lesson 5   Name Explosions

Your alarm clock didn't go off on time this morning, your car broke down on the way to work, your report cards are due in the office, and since it is raining your kids will have to have an indoor recess. What you need is an easy-to-present art lesson that your class will enjoy and that will give you time to swallow a couple of aspirins so that you can relax for a minute.

Believe me, more than one teacher has had reason to thank this *Name Explosion* lesson for the time it gave them just to pull themselves together!

YOU NEED:

paper, pencils, and crayons

Figure 1-5A

TO PRESENT:

1.   Invite your kids to draw their names in "fat letters" as suggested in Figure 1-5B. Overlapping of letters is to be encouraged.

2.   Once the name has been drawn and colored in, have each child draw a line around the name as shown in Figure 1-5C.

3.   And around *that* other lines are drawn, spreading outwards like ripples in a pond. (See Figure 1-5A.) Your kids will get the idea immediately.

Now—go take your aspirin!

Figure 1-5B

Figure 1-5C

Lesson 6   Giving the Victorians a Hand

If there is one area in which the Victorians excelled it was in their penmanship. While the lesson that follows does not pretend to be a crash course in this Victorian art form, it will show your kids how to make a pretty fair imitation that is not only fun to do but really quite impressive in its own way!

YOU NEED:

scrap paper and lined paper
pencils and rulers or *Straight-Edges* (see Glossary)
pens optional

Figure 1-6A

TO PRESENT:

1.   Explain to your kids that the two-fold secret to this kind of writing is: 1) neatness and 2) the shaded downstroke. Show on the chalkboard what is meant by upstrokes and downstrokes by using a lower case cursive "s." The downstroke, you explain, is that part of the letter drawn as your hand comes down (toward your body). See Figures 1-6B and 1-6C. In the last Figure the downstroke is thickened or *shaded*.

2.   Explain also that in some of the letters such as the lower case "z" the shading goes from thin to thick to thin again (see Figure 1-6D), while the shading in other letters such as the lower case "t" and "p" has abrupt starts and stops. (See Figures 1-6E and 1-6F.)

Figure 1-6B

Figure 1-6C

Figure 1-6D

Figure 1-6E

Figure 1-6F

3.   After your kids have practiced this concept on scrap paper so that they understand the process, have them join you in this simple exercise:

PRELIMINARY EXERCISE

In your best handwriting, write out a word or two on the chalkboard for your kids to copy on their lined paper. Then, when everybody is ready, work together in darkening the downstrokes as shown in Figure 1-6A.

Supplementary Information

The primary difference between Victorian script and orthodox calligraphy is that the Victorians wrote in what is called a *round hand script*, which is a true cursive style with joined letters. *Calligraphy,* on the other hand, is an angular, Gothic-looking, chisel-point pen script composed almost entirely of downstrokes. (See Figures 1-6G and 1-6H.)

Figure 1-6G

CONCLUDING ACTIVITY

Once your kids understand how to do it, your job is over, for on their own they'll find enough uses for this lettering style to keep themselves busy for some time to come!

Figure 1-6H

Lesson 7   The Victorian Revisited

In the previous lesson I showed you how to gracefully shade your downstrokes to make a pretty fair imitation of a Victorian round hand script. If you enjoyed that lesson, wait until you see what happens when you begin to apply the same principle to decorative line drawings!

YOU NEED:

pencils and paper
pens optional

Figure 1-7A

Figure 1-7B

Figure 1-7C

TO PRESENT:

Victorian penmanship goes hand in hand with another popular Victorian art form: the shaded line drawing. While I do not pretend to have mastered this art form, the illustrations above and below should give you some idea of the decorative possibilities.

1. Have your kids prepare some kind of a continuous line drawing as shown in Figure 1-7B.*

2. Then, using the information learned in the previous lesson, shade the downstrokes so that they look something like those shown here in Figure 1-7C.

3. So why waste any more time? Just tell your class what I've told you, pass out the pencils and paper, and let them go to work!

Lesson 8   Fold-Outs

Since all kids love surprises, these *Fold-Outs* are—by design—first class child-pleasers!

YOU NEED:

6″ × 12″ drawing paper

pencils and crayons (or any other suitable art media)

PREPARATIONS:

Fold-Outs are pictures drawn on folded paper in such a way as to accommodate a dramatic change of image. While the exact positioning of the fold is not crucial, those of you who have worked extensively with kids know that it is far easier to hand out prefolded papers than to try to explain to a

---

*I cheated; I used not one but *two* continuous lines. But who cares? I am not Victorian, our kids are not Victorian, so if we break a Victorian rule now and then, who's to tell? What is important here is that these things are fun to do and kids like to do them. And what better recommendation can you give than that?

young audience that "the exact positioning of the fold is not crucial"!

What I do is this: after cutting up 12″ × 18″ drawing paper into 6″ × 12″ lengths, I use the metal-edged side of my paper cutter to help me fold my papers quickly and crisply. The folding instructions given in Figures 1-8A and 1-8B are as good as any for starters.

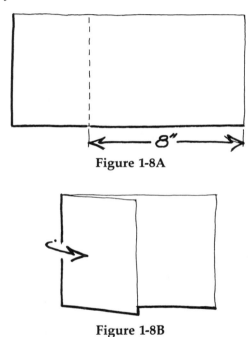

Figure 1-8A

Figure 1-8B

To complete your preparations see Figures 1-8C and 1-8D for suggestions for making up a sample *Fold-Out* of your own to show your kids.

Figure 1-8C   **Figure 1-8D**

TO PRESENT:

Once you have followed the instructions given above, there is not much more to do. Simply pass out the prefolded paper, show them your sample so that they'll get the idea, and then let them go to work!

Here, in the illustrations that follow, are some sample Fold-Out suggestions. (See Figures 1-8E and F, 1-8G and H, 1-8I and J.)

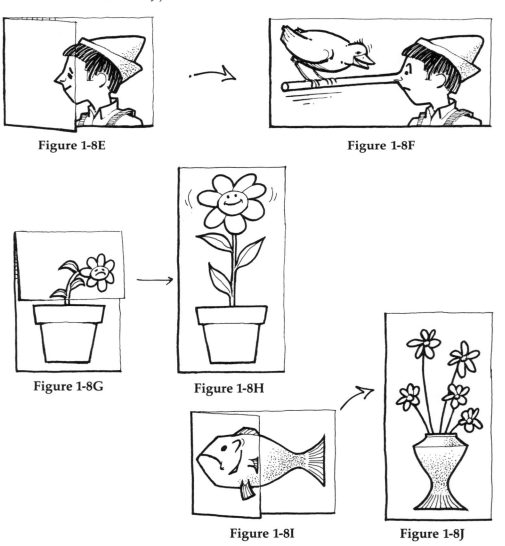

Figure 1-8E   **Figure 1-8F**

Figure 1-8G   **Figure 1-8H**

Figure 1-8I   **Figure 1-8J**

Lesson 9   **Holiday Street**

When I first devised this pre-Christmas lesson plan I knew I had a good one. How good? Even I was suprised with the kind of hearty reception given my *Holiday Street*. Try it!

YOU NEED:

> gray and yellow construction paper (9″ × 24″ is a perfect size but smaller paper works well too!)
>
> pencil and black crayon
>
> white chalk
>
> stapler
>
> single-edged razor blade or hobby knife and a cardboard cutting surface.

Figure 1-9A

TO PRESENT:

1. Explain to your kids that at dusk colors fade away and the world becomes gray. Invite your kids to use their pencils and the gray paper to sketch out a street at Christmas time. Explain that later on the lights will be turned on in the houses and buildings, and that snow has been predicted for later in the evening.

2. Once your kids have sketched out the basic idea have them finish the picture using nothing but a black crayon outline. When the outline is finished (or whenever you are ready to begin to use your razor blade to cut out their

windows), have your kids line up so that you can "turn on their lights."

3.   Once the windows have been cut out, have them place their gray paper on top of their yellow paper to witness the instantaneous end to the evening's blackout. Once the two top corners are stapled invite your kids to draw whatever they wish behind the illuminated windows. They'll love it!

4.   For a great finish, pass out the chalk so that the predicted snow can arrive in time to complete the festivities!

Lesson 10   Weave and Decorate Designs

Once when I was giving a paper weaving lesson to a large class of first graders, the limited time slot in which I had to work was such that I could do little more than deliver rapid-fire instructions and attend to the assembly line distribution of supplies. I did not even have time to explain to this group what weaving was—which was a mistake—for with five, six, and seven year olds everything has to be *something* or it is next to worthless.

"Is it a checkerboard?" ("No.") "Is it a placemat?" ("Not really, it's just *weaving*.") While I was being bombarded with these and similar concerns, a little girl with a clear, bell-like voice saved the day by asking one simple, straightforward question. "Mr. Baer," she asked, "is it all right if we *decorate* it?"

Of course it was all right! The idea was an inspired one for soon all of the kids were busy filling in the woven squares with all kinds of personal touches.

Now I don't know why in a kid's mind a decorated weaving should be more of a "something" than a nondecorated weaving, but I suspect that it has something to do with the difference between the cool, impersonal beauty of the woven color and the warmth and individuality of the direct statement.

In any case, these *Weave and Decorate Designs* are *always* unqualified successes. You'll love them!

YOU NEED:

12" × 18" manila drawing paper

2" × 18" strips of white drawing or construction paper (three each)

assorted colors of construction paper in the following sizes:

2" × 18" (three of each color)

2" × 12" (four of a second color and four of still another)

paste, crayons, and stapler

Figure 1-10A

TO PRESENT:

1. Begin by having your kids lay down their long strips upon the manila paper as shown in Figure 1-10B. Then have them place a small amount of paste at one end only to "tack" this assembly together until you have time to anchor each strip with a staple.

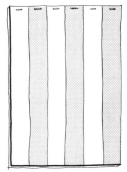

Figure 1-10B

2.   Once all the paper "looms" have been assembled, direct your class to "pick up all of the long white strips in one hand." When they have done so, have them insert one of the shorter strips crosswise under the white. The white strips are then dropped and the long colored ones are raised so that an alternate short piece can be placed under the long colored pieces. Once your kids have the idea, the only help that many of them will need will be help in squeezing their weaving together to make a tighter weave. When they are done, have them paste down all of the loose ends or place a single staple through each end of the last woven short piece of paper.

3.   As for the decorating part, few of your kids will need any further suggestions. Just let 'em go! (See Figure 1-10A.)

Lesson 11   Just Truckin'

Some art activities demand a great deal of thought and preparation. *Just Truckin'* is a quickie that requires a minimum of preparation and is as foolproof a lesson plan as you'll ever find!

YOU NEED:

construction paper in the following colors and sizes:
   6" × 9", 3" × 4½" and 2¼" × 3" "truck" colors
   2" squares black
   small scraps of white
   4¾" × 8" truck sign color (optional)
12" × 18" drawing paper
paste, pencils, scissors, and crayons

TO PRESENT:

1.   Have your kids assemble their three colored rectangles into a basic truck shape and paste it to the drawing paper as shown here in Figure 1-11B.

Figure 1-11A

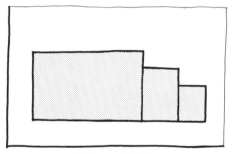

Figure 1-11B

2.   Large, square-filling, "wheel" circles are then drawn on the black paper, cut out, and pasted in place.

3.   Hub caps and a window for the cab are made from the scrap white and they too are pasted in place.

4.   Now all you have to do is invite your kids to finish their pictures in any way they desire. *Your* job is done!

Lesson 12   The Leprechaun Gold Bar Mystery

Paper currency occasionally tears and when this happens most people simply patch it together with a strip of cellophane tape and pass it on. Be advised, however, that the U.S. Treasury Department is extremely vigilant in these matters, for there is a little known (but diabolically clever) currency swindle that seemingly makes cut-and-restored bills go farther than they honestly should!

The scheme works like this: the swindler lays out, say, ten $100 bills and then carefully cuts them along the line indicated in Figure 1-12A.

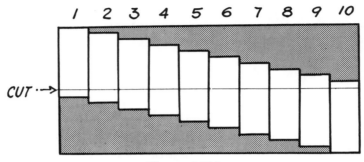

Figure 1-12A

Now all the crook has to do is to push the lower parts of the trimmed bills to the right as shown in Figure 1-12B, and—presto! he automatically receives a free $100 bill for his efforts!

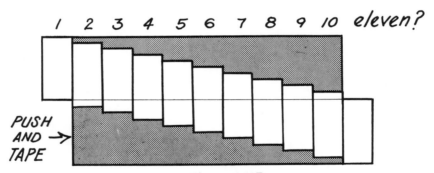

Figure 1-12B

You, on the other hand, have *two* choices: you can do the same thing, tape $100 bills together and tangle with the law, or you can do what I do and use this "principle of concealed distribution"* to captivate kids. Here is one way to put this knowledge to *good* use:

---

*Martin Gardner's terminology.

YOU NEED:

construction paper:
>   12″ × 18″ dark green (or any other good background color)
>   12″ × 18″ back-up sheet (any color)
>   nine 1½″ × 5″ yellow-orange (or any other related color that can be used to represent gold)

ruler

paste or glue

scissors (or paper cutter)

paper clips

PREPARATIONS:

1.   Fold the 12″ × 18″ green sheet lengthwise; unfold. Using a ruler, divide the creased line into twelve 1½″ segments as shown here in Figure 1-12C.

2.   Paste the nine 1½″ × 5″ gold bars as shown in Figure 1-12D. Cut on the long center fold and paste lower section to back-up sheet as shown.

3.   Cut off 1½″ × 6″ rectangle as shown in Figure 1-12E, and use the paper clips to reunite the whole assembly as shown here in Figure 1-12F.

4.   *Now*—you're ready to begin!

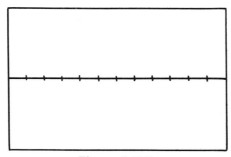

Figure 1-12C

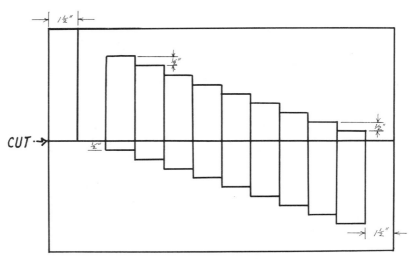

Figure 1-12D

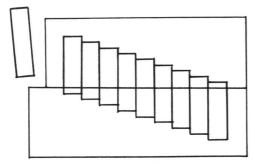

Figure 1-12E

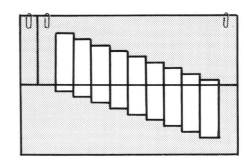

Figure 1-12F

TO PRESENT:

Instead of telling your kids stories of dishonest currency transactions, tell them instead the story of night watchman O'Flanagan, the aged Leprechaun, whose job it was to keep count of the colony's nine bar gold supply. (When showing the first gold bar assembly [Figure 1-12F] to your kids, have them count these bars aloud in unison.)

It seems that one evening as O'Flanagan was making his count he quite accidentally dropped all ten bars to the floor where they shattered: some of these precious bars broke in half, some in quarters and some just along the ends. (At this point in your story remove the paper clips to allow the illustrated gold also to "shatter.")

Not knowing what else to do at this point, the old Leprechaun knelt down and very carefully glued those bars back together again. (Reassemble your visual aid with paper clips as shown in Figure 1-12G.) When his gluing was complete and he stood up to appraise his handiwork, he discovered something *very* peculiar. O'Flanagan counted once, he counted twice, but no matter how many times he counted he still ended up with *ten* gold bars: which was, of course, one more gold bar than he had dropped!* (Show your kids the rearranged bars as shown here in Figure 1-12G.)

Now—ask your kids to explain *that!*

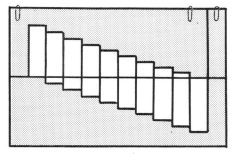

Figure 1-12G

Lesson 13　　　　**Bugging Out**

If you and your kids enjoyed the *Leprechaun Gold Bar Mystery* in the previous lesson—you're going to *revel* in this one!

YOU NEED:

6″ × 15″ pattern-weight paperboard

---

*A tongue-in-cheek ending to this story: "Not knowing what to do with this extra gold bar, the old watchman stored it in his room, which explains why—to this day— all the Little People for miles around still refer to this popular nightime spot as O'Flanagan's Leprechaun Bar Room."

12″ × 18″ drawing paper

pencils, scissors, and crayons or other art media

Figure 1-13A

PREPARATION:

Prepare your paperboard patterns exactly as shown in Figure 1-13B.

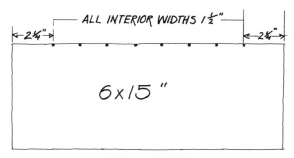

Figure 1-13B

TO PRESENT:

1.   Have your kids fold their 12″ × 18″ papers in half lengthwise, unfold, and then use their prepared patterns to lay out their 12″ × 18″ paper exactly as shown in Figure 1-13C.

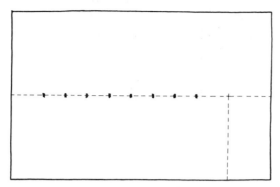

Figure 1-13C

2.   Now comes the only tricky part to this whole illusion: explain to your kids that they are going to design four "bugs," and while the detailed features of each of these bugs will be a matter of taste, certain overall rules must be followed if this illusion is going to succeed. (Since some adjustments may be desired later, advise your kids to sketch out these bugs *lightly* in pencil. There will be plenty of time for "finishing" later.)

The "first bug" listed below refers to the left-hand bug in Figure 1-13D, the "second" to the second from the left, etc.

First Bug. Position this first bug above the first pair of dots in such a way that only a small tail-end segment extends over the middle line.

Figure 1-13D

Second Bug. Position this second bug so that a medium-sized tail-end segment extends over the middle line.

Third Bug. Design the extending rear-end segment of
this bug a little larger than the last.

Final Bug. Position this bug so that only the head is left
extending above the middle line.

3.   Once the bugs have been sketched in, have your
kids cut their drawings apart as shown in Figure 1-13E. *Save
all parts.*

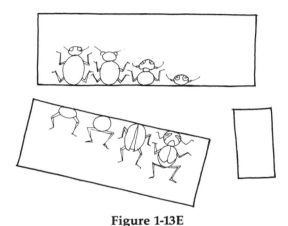

Figure 1-13E

4.   Now comes the magic, for—if your classes are like
my classes—by the time they have finished with their
scissors, some of your kids will already have discovered the
magical properties of these three pieces of paper: assembled
one way there are *four* bugs, assembled another and the bug
population increases by one! (See Figures 1-13F and 1-13G.)

Figure 1-13F

Figure 1-13G

5. Once your kids have been introduced to the "magic," recommend this old wizard's advice to decorate their bugs in some kind of a limited color scheme. *Then—* step back and let 'em go!

Lesson 14   The Mountain-Rangers

The secret to many good lesson plans often rests on nothing more complicated than a good old-fashioned "starter"*: a simple, easy-to-present attention grabber that allows a great deal of learning to take place in a game-like atmosphere. The *Mountain-Rangers* is this kind of a lesson.

YOU NEED:

pencils and 8½" square lightweight paper (newsprint, duplicating, or mimeo stock will do just fine!)

TO PRESENT:

While the idea behind the Mountain-Ranger is entertaining enough to stand alone, I prefer to use it as a basis for a drawing lesson. Here's how I do it with older kids:

---

*If you are interested in other "starter" lessons, I devoted a whole chapter to this concept in *Art and Kids* (Parker, 1981).

Figure 1-14A

Figure 1-14B

Figure 1-14C

Figure 1-14D

PART ONE: THE WORK

I explain to my kids that the first part of this lesson is going to be work, and that the last part is going to be fun; and that we will begin this lesson by learning how adults draw the "side-view" face.*

The Eye

Like the artists of ancient Egypt, most kids draw an all-purpose, symbolic eye that is used for both front and profile views. While there is nothing wrong with this schema, kids (particularly older kids) are always interested in seeing how an adult might approach this same problem. (See Figures 1-14A through 1-14D.)

The Nose

Noses drawn by kids are often large, beak-like, and severed from the face by a line. (See Figure 1-14E.)

Here are a few pointers for drawing a nose in adult language. (See Figure 1-14F.)

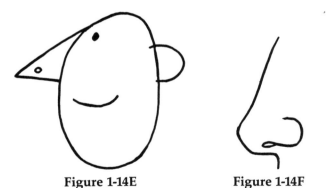

Figure 1-14E   **Figure 1-14F**

---

*"Drawing the human face in profile" would be a more accurate use of the English language but I teach *kids*, not *Englishmen*.

The Ear

For a three-step approach to an adult ear, see Figures 1-14G, 1-14H, and 1-14I.

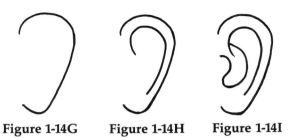

Figure 1-14G **Figure 1-14H** **Figure 1-14I**

PART TWO: THE FUN

1. Have your kids use their pencils to draw a light line down the center of the paper. (See Figure 1-14J.)

2. Draw a four-peak mountain range ending on this penciled line as shown in Figure 1-14K.

3. Turn this paper one-quarter turn to the left, and complete the surprise profile! (See Figures 1-14L and 1-14M.)

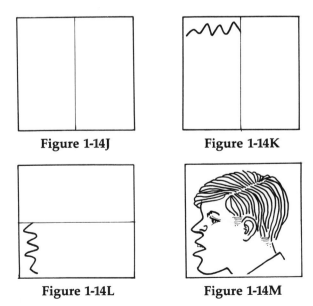

Figure 1-14J **Figure 1-14K**

Figure 1-14L **Figure 1-14M**

SUPPLEMENTARY ILLUSTRATIONS

Here are a few results demonstrating the variety of human expressions that can be found in these mountains. (See Figures 1-14N through 1-14Q.)

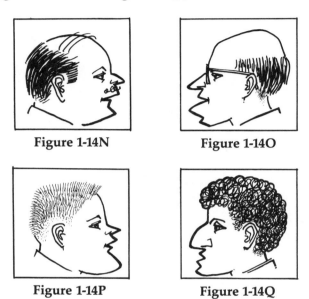

Figure 1-14N   **Figure 1-14O**

Figure 1-14P   **Figure 1-14Q**

Lesson 15   Skating at Foil Pond

It was not until recently that I began to explore some of the off-beat ways in which common kitchen foil can be used to dress up an art lesson. Here, for example, is as easy a way to put life into a midwinter lesson as any you'll ever find!

YOU NEED:

12″ × 18″ white drawing paper
roll of 12″ kitchen foil
4½″ × 12″ lightweight paperboard
6″ × 9″ drawing paper
paste, pencils, scissors, and crayons

Figure 1-15A

TO PRESENT:

1.   On the 4½" × 12" paperboard have your kids draw a large imperfect oval.

2.   While your class is busy drawing their ovals and cutting them out, *your* job is to walk around the room with the box of kitchen foil and to tear off strips of foil just a fraction larger in size than the paperboard ovals. When delivering this foil, place it shiny side down in front of each child with the instructions not to turn this foil over.

3.   When the ovals are cut out, have your kids place them on top of their foil and then have them turn the edges of the foil inward to contain the oval. Then, with scissors, trim much of this foil back so that there is a good deal of paperboard exposed as shown in Figure 1-15B.

4.   Paste is then applied to the exposed paperboard and then this whole sub-assembly is turned over and pasted onto the bottom of the white drawing paper as shown here in Figure 1-15C.

Figure 1-15B

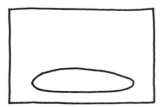

Figure 1-15C

5.   The rest is easy. Have your kids use their 6″ × 9″ paper to draw, color, and cut out skaters (or sliders) and paste them to the white drawing paper as shown in Figure 1-15A. The rest of the picture is then left to the wintery imaginations of your kids; just turn them loose and let them go!

Lesson 16   **Classroom Time**

One way to quicken the tempo of an art activity is to find a way to bring the subject closer to home. In the activity that follows, not only do we bring the lesson into the classroom but the classroom into the lesson!

YOU NEED:

6″ × 9″ and 12″ × 18″ drawing paper

paste, pencils, scissors, and crayons

plus: the additional materials described in the paragraph
    below.

Figure 1-16A

PREPARATIONS:

The secret to the success of this activity lies in the degree to which the pictured room resembles the classroom in which the lesson is being conducted. To assist in this matter you can give your kids a head start in the right direction by giving them one or more colored paper pieces precut to represent particular room features such as doors, chalkboards, etc. And *that* will be all the preparation needed to get this lesson off to a flying start!

TO PRESENT:

1.	Pass out the 12″ × 18″ drawing paper and the cut-out room features discussed under *Preparations* (above). Have your kids paste these in place.

2.	After the floor line has been drawn, the whole picture is then finished with an eye for existing detail.

3.	And finally, when Step 2 is well underway, pass out the 6″ × 9″ paper so that your kids can either: (1) make a picture of themselves, or (2) make a picture of their teacher. This picture is then colored, cut out, and pasted into position!* (See Figure 1-16A.)

Lesson 17 *Nine*-Part Flip-Flops

In one of my previous books** I presented two Flip-Flopping activities based upon a simple six-part format. (See Figures 1-17A and 1-17B.)

Figure 1-17A

Figure 1-17B

*This would be as good a time as any to differentiate between the *floor line* and the *floor area*. In other words, explain to your kids the difference between having their figures standing on the floor and standing on the baseboard!

**Paste, Pencils, Scissors and Crayons* (Parker, 1979).

Here are some more top quality Flip-Flopping ideas that bring into full focus some of the rich and varied surprises that can be offered by this versatile classroom entertainer.

If there are nine different child-pleasing pairs of images in every six-part Flip-Flop, how many picture changes can you expect to find in a nine-part invention? I once counted twenty-seven—but maybe I missed a few!

ACTIVITY NUMBER ONE: HEAD-FLOPS

YOU NEED:

6″ × 12″ pattern-weight paperboard *Measuring Strips* (See Glossary)

12″ × 18″ drawing paper

pencils, scissors, and crayons

TO PRESENT:

1.   Have your kids fold their 12″ × 18″ paper in half lengthwise, unfold, and then fold the long sides into the middle. Unfold and cut off one of these long quarters as indicated by shading in Figure 1-17C.

2.   The Measuring Strips are used to divide these papers into horizontal thirds. Cut on the heavy lines indicated in Figure 1-17D.

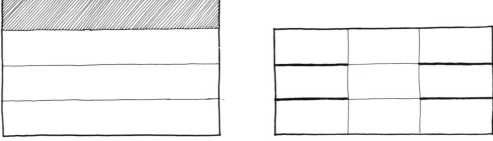

Figure 1-17C   **Figure 1-17D**

3.   The rest is easy. Have your kids draw the central part of the head (ears, eyes, and nose) in the middle panel,

the mouth and chin in the lower, and the forehead and hair in the top panel. Flip-Flop sections to add feature changes and continue until done. (See Figures 1-17E, 1-17F, and 1-17G.)

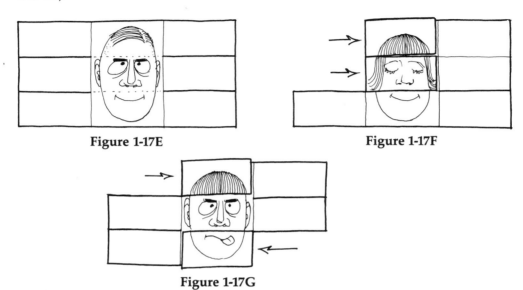

Figure 1-17E   **Figure 1-17F**

Figure 1-17G

4.   And for those who finish early, have them turn their papers over for there are still enough rectangles left over to do it again!

ACTIVITY NUMBER TWO: CREATURE-FLOPS

YOU NEED:

The needs list of the previous lesson plus 4″ × 18″ Measuring Strips.*

TO PRESENT:

1.   With pencil and the 6″ × 12″ Measuring Strips, have your kids divide their papers into three parts as shown in Figure 1-17H.

---

*See Glossary.

Figure 1-17H   **Figure 1-17I**

2.   The 4″ × 18″ Measuring Strips are used for dividing the same paper into thirds from the other direction. (See Figure 1-17I.) Cut on the heavy lines shown in Figure 1-17J.

3.   Once your kids understand the *Head-Flops* of the previous activity, this one should go smoothly. Draw a head and neck in the first part, the front part of the body in the second, and back legs (and tail) in the third as suggested in Figure 1-17J.

Figure 1-17K illustrates the *Creature-Flops* in action!

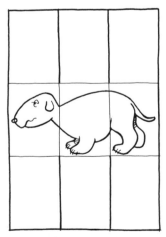

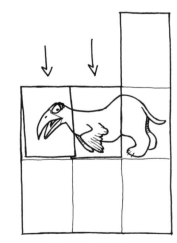

Figure 1-17J   **Figure 1-17K**

Lesson 18   Hula Holiday

While you may or may not consider this lesson appropriate for *your* classroom, I assure you that this Hawaiian dancer has been the star performer of many a memorable Cub Scout orgy!

YOU NEED:

8½″ × 11″ lightweight paper (duplicating or mimeo supplies work well here)

9″ × 12″ black construction paper

stapler

flashlight

Figure 1-18A

TO PRESENT:

1.   Have your kids draw a full-length silhouette of a hula dancer on the black paper and then cut it out. (See Figure 1-18B.)

2.   Staple this figure top and bottom to the lightweight

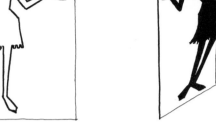

Figure 1-18B   **Figure 1-18C**

paper in such a way that the hips of the figure bow out from the surface as shown in Figure 1-18C.

3.   Turn off the room lights. The blank side of the white paper is then shown to the audience while a moving flashlight beam is played on the silhouette side. The realistic and yet highly comic gyrations of this Hawaiian dancer are *always* a great success!

Lesson 19   Octet for Crayons and Kids

When I sit down to make out my lesson plans, my teaching experience generally provides me with some realistic expectations about the way a new lesson will be received. When I first devised this particular lesson plan, my gut feeling was that while *Octet for Crayons and Kids* would make an acceptable lesson, it was considerably less than my best effort. I couldn't have been more wrong in my judgment. For reasons that are not apparent to anyone but kids, *Octet for Crayons and Kids* has turned out to be a highly popular activity that invariably generates great interest and profound creativity. Try it and you'll see what I mean!

YOU NEED:

    practice paper
    12″ × 18″ drawing paper
    pencils and crayons

Figure 1-19A

TO PRESENT:

INTRODUCTORY LESSON

1.   Begin with a "do as I do" design lesson: you at the chalkboard, your kids with pencils and practice paper. I generally begin with what the kids call the "cinchy" ones: circles, squares, and triangles followed by hearts, diamonds, clubs, and spades.

Incidentally, a club can be drawn with three hearts and a stem; a spade as an inverted heart with stem. (See Figures 1-19B through 1-19F.)

2.   Once you have also had your kids draw other "cinchy" ones like five-pointed and six-pointed stars, introduce them to the idea of making their own symmetrical ("same on both sides") designs. See Figures 1-19G and 1-19H for examples.

Figure 1-19B

Figure 1-19C

Figure 1-19D

Figure 1-19E

Figure 1-19F

Figure 1-19G

Figure 1-19H

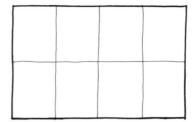

Figure 1-19I

CONCLUDING ACTIVITY

1.   Have your kids fold their 12″ × 18″ drawing paper in half widthwise, unfold, and then fold the sides into the center. Open up and fold once lengthwise. (See Figure 1-19I.)

2.   And that's it. Just point out to your kids that their papers are all in readiness to receive eight different creative designs. And if your kids are like my kids, I assure you that you'll be both surprised and delighted with the quality of the work that this activity generates!

Lesson 20   Little Guys

There is always a certain amount of risk involved in introducing a new lesson, and a certain amount of accompanying anxiety. When I invented these *Little Guys,* the first class to try it out was a lively group of third graders. Whatever fears I may have entertained were soon proven unfounded for once this project got underway it was unstoppable. Twenty-four hours later these kids were still stealing time away from their other subjects to add to their cast of these engaging, big-mouthed puppets!

YOU NEED:

two sheets of 6″ × 9″ drawing paper
1⅛″ × 6″ scrap paper
tape
paste (or stapler)
pencils, scissors, and crayons

Figure 1-20A

TO PRESENT:

1. Have your kids fold one of their 6″ × 9″ papers in half widthwise. Unfold and fold one of the short ends in to touch the center fold. Unfold. (See Figures 1-20B and 1-20C.)

2. Take this last fold and refold it in the opposite direction to give it a new "memory." (See Figure 1-20D.)

3. Bring this "brainwashed" fold to the middle fold to make one more fold as shown here in Figure 1-20E. Keeping the paper in this folded position, have your kids draw in any kind of a face that (1) fills the paper and (2) uses the folded

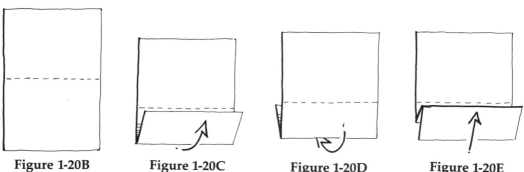

Figure 1-20B   **Figure 1-20C**   **Figure 1-20D**   **Figure 1-20E**

line as the lip line. Note in Figure 1-20F how the ears are placed *above* the lip line.

4.   Once this face has been drawn and colored to suit the child, it is to be cut out while the paper is still in its folded position. Once the cutting is complete, the head might look something like the one illustrated in Figure 1-20G. The inside of the mouth can then be colored in—with or without tongue and teeth—as shown in Figure 1-20H.

Figure 1-20F   **Figure 1-20G**   **Figure 1-20H**

5.   The other 6″ × 9″ paper is for making the body, which can then be pasted (or stapled) to the head as shown in Figure 1-20A.

OPERATING INSTRUCTIONS

For supreme ease of manipulation, the following behind-the-scene improvements will be well worth the additional effort expended:

1.   Have your kids roll their 1⅛″ × 6″ paper strips around the ends of their index fingers and tape. (See Figure 1-20I.)

2.   In turn, tape this "finger-holder" to the back top of the puppet's mouth and to the back of the head as shown here in Figure 1-20J.

Figure 1-20I   **Figure 1-20J**

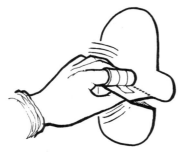

Figure 1-20K

3. To operate: simply place the index finger in the finger-holder and the thumb directly below as shown in Figure 1-20K and use! (Your kids will show you how!)

Lesson 21   A Classroom Strip Show

I designed this lesson in response to a reading teacher's request for me to do something with "sequencing." It took me only a moment or two to realize that *sequencing* and comic strip making were one and the same thing, and only another moment's contemplation to visualize how this lesson could be transformed into a showpiece.

Given a choice between being a Rembrandt and being a comic strip artist, most kids (and, I suspect, most adults as well) would take the comic route anytime. Comics are easier to draw, financially more profitable, and often immensely entertaining.

And just as kids love comics, they love this *Classroom Strip Show!*

YOU NEED:

3¼" × 4" drawing paper

4" × 18" black construction paper

paste or glue

pencils, pens, or fine-line markers

Figure 1-21A

TO PRESENT:

While no elaborate instructions are needed, this lesson (like many other concept lessons) will go more easily if you can prepare some kind of a homemade example ahead of time.

The only further instructions that your kids might need to be reminded of are: (1) that their comic strip should be designed so that their story can be told in *four* frames, and (2) that each of these frames is designed to be seen horizontally.*

Then turn your kids loose on their assigned task. When they are done with their first comic strip, have them paste their panels onto the black construction paper as shown in Figure 1-21A. Then—make some more!

---

*I hope that the reader understands that there are many nuances to teaching a good lesson that, for matters of brevity, I sometimes leave unsaid. For example:

Once a lesson like this gets underway, sooner or later some kid is going to complain that this four-part panel format is much too short for what has to be said. The question then becomes, "Is it all right if I hitch on more paper?" Of course it's all right; I'm teaching sequencing—not dictatorially preparing art work to fill assigned space. Let these kids do what they want to do with this adventure in sequencing, and your lesson will be all the better for this added enrichment!

As to words like *horizontal, vertical, widthwise* and *lengthwise,* I hope that none of my readers suppose that I would be so ill-advised as to expect kids to understand this kind of adult language. In the case asterisked above, I would probably say something like "Turn your paper the *long way* to work on it." If, on the other hand, I wanted the paper to be used in a vertical position, I would say something like "Turn your paper to the *up-and-down* position to work on it." Or a kid might use this last term in a sentence such as "Is it all right if I have my whole comic strip going up-and-down?"

And the answer to this last question is "Of course. *You're* the artist!"

Lesson 22   From My House to Yours

Some lesson plans work best if they begin with a flying start. This lesson is one of these. While *From My House to Yours* will demand a little preparation time on your part, the results will be well worth the trouble!

YOU NEED:

12" × 18" pastel-colored construction paper

12" × 18" manila or white drawing paper

6" × 9" colored construction paper in assorted colors

(one) yard stick

(one) sheet of 12" × 18" pattern-weight paperboard

(one) single-edged razor blade or hobby knife

(one) piece of desk-protecting cardboard

(one) stapler

paste, pencils, scissors, and crayons

Figure 1-22A

PREPARATIONS:

1. Using the width of your yardstick as your pattern, pencil in a floor line on each of the 12″ × 18″ pastel papers. (See Figure 1-22B.)

2. Repeat this same operation on the 12″ × 18″ pattern-weight paperboard but on this sheet (only) cut off the floor area. (See Figure 1-22C.)

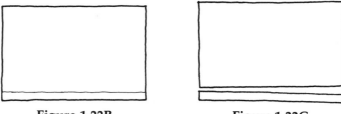

Figure 1-22B   **Figure 1-22C**

3. Then, using this same paperboard, draw in a door and a window as suggested in Figure 1-22D. Cut away the shaded areas.

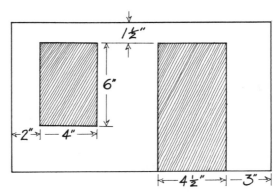

Figure 1-22D

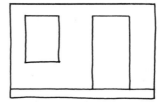

Figure 1-22E

4. Trace this pattern on all of the 12″ × 18″ pastel papers to complete the room plan as shown here in Figure 1-22E.

TO PRESENT:

1. Pass out the sheets of pastel room paper with the instructions to poke a hole in the middle of the window and to cut out the rest with their scissors. While your kids are busily employed "breaking windows," invite them to come up to your desk—one at a time—so that you can use your razor blade or hobby knife to open up three sides of the door. (See Figure 1-22A.)

3. While all of this activity is going on you can explain to your kids that what they have in front of them is an interior of a house (your house, their house, anybody's house). This house, of course, needs extensive remodeling and decorating. (Baseboards? Door knobs? Window on door? Curtains? Drapes? Carpet?)

While most of this remodeling and decorating can be done in crayon, things like curtains or drapes will need colored paper. For this you introduce the 6″ × 9″ assorted colored paper with the invitation to help themselves when ready. Three long strips cut from the 6″ × 9″ paper can easily be assembled to look like the drapes shown in Figure 1-22A.

4. Then, while your kids are busy "fixin' up" their houses, your job is to wander around the room stapling the drawing paper to the back of the room paper. Staple only the two top corners so that—when the time comes—your kids only have to lift up the bottom of their room papers to work on their outside environments. When the last background sheet has been stapled, *your* work is done. Go design your own environment—they don't need *you* any more!

Lesson 23   Assorted Rainbow Sunsets

One of my more memorable mailorder purchases occurred when I ordered (or thought I had ordered) *assorted* colored construction paper and instead received *rainbow*. The two are *not* identical. "Assorted" means that the packages contain paper of many different hues, values, and intensities. "Rainbow" paper also comes in many hues values and intensities but all of these nuances are to be found on *each* sheet!

In any case, here I was waiting for an order of "assorted" and in comes a delivery of "rainbow." Send this paper back or use it? I used it—and the results were spectacular!

Here's how:

YOU NEED:

construction paper:
  12" × 18" black
  12" × 18" rainbow (*not* "assorted")
  4½" × 6" yellow
paste, pencils, scissors, and possibly even a black crayon

Figure 1-23A

TO PRESENT:

1.   Explain to your kids that one of the best times of the day is at sunset when the sky is a glowing palette of color

and the horizon is by contrast dark and preparing for night. With that, invite your kids to draw their skyline of houses, buildings, etc. and when done to cut this skyline out and paste it to the sunset paper.

2.   While they are busy doing this, pass out the yellow "window" paper so that your kids can snip out rectangles that can be pasted down to turn on some of the lights that are always seen at sunset. The results will be just as you might expect—glorious! (See Figure 1-23A.)

Lesson 24   Getting Deeper into the Book Business

Most people haven't the slightest idea about how to prepare copy for publication. And why should they? Only a small percentage of our population will ever become involved in writing, illustrating, publishing, or printing.

On the other hand, when I have used the following lesson to explain the rudiments of the business to kids, most of them find this introductory exposure fascinating. And why shouldn't they—this end of the book business is just plain *fun!*

Figure 1-24A

YOU NEED:

8½″ × 11″ lightweight white paper (duplicator or mimeo supplies work very well here)

stapler (the classroom kind that unhinges and opens up for tacking purposes)

a double thickness of corrugated cardboard

pencils

crayons or other art materials

4½″ × 11¼″ pastel-colored construction paper

TO PRESENT:

1.   Have your kids fold their 8½″ × 11″ paper in half lengthwise. Keeping this paper folded, fold it once again as shown in Figure 1-24B.

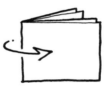

Figure 1-24B

2.   Unfold and place this paper on the desk with the long fold up as shown in Figure 1-24C. Then have your kids copy the page numbers *exactly* as shown. Note that some of the page numbers are upside down.

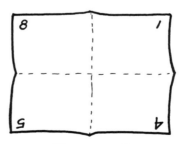

Figure 1-24C

3. Turn this paper over so that the *back* of page one is at the upper left-hand corner. Now copy the page numbers here as shown in Figure 1-24D. Once again bring attention to the fact that some of these numbers are upside down and should be written that way.

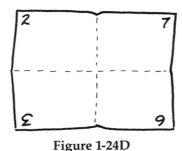

Figure 1-24D

4. Now invite your kids to write and illustrate their own eight-page booklet following the exact eight-page format as it appears on their prepared papers. To the puzzled cries of this-doesn't-seem-right-to-me and how-come-everything-is-all-mixed-up? answer, "You'll see, you'll see!"

Those children who finish this task early can fold their pastel paper in half and start working on their front cover while the rest of the kids are still busy with their illustrated text. (And the real speed demons who finish *that* can always be shuttled off to the task of designing the back cover—complete with the author's picture, etc.!)

5. When the main body of your author/illustrator group have finished the first part of their assignment, have them refold their papers lengthwise as shown in Figure 1-24E. Then fold again as demonstrated in Figure 1-24F so that page 8 is turned to face the rear.

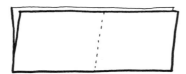

Figure 1-24E

Figure 1-24F

ASSEMBLING INSTRUCTIONS

Now comes the only real bottleneck in this whole lesson, and the solution to this matter I must leave to *your* organizational skills. Here's what needs to be done:

1.   The book and its cover must be placed on a double thickness of corrugated cardboard where two staples are shot through its spine. (Figure 1-24G.) The book is then inverted and the upright ends of the penetrated staples are turned down with a hard, blunt instrument (such as the end of a ruler). (See Figure 1-24H.)

Figure 1-24G

Figure 1-24H

2.   The booklet is then closed and trimmed along the bottom edge with a paper cutter. With this one quick stroke the pages are freed from the prison of the locked packet. Watch the faces of your kids as they open their booklets to

Figure 1-24I

discover that their jumbled pages have been—quite mysteriously—rearranged into proper sequence. What may have begun as an upside-down/inside-out way of working has been met with instant vindication, leaving in its wake a rational, exciting and resounding classroom success! (Figure 1-24I.)

ONCE AROUND THE CALENDAR

Cats and pumpkins for Halloween, Santa and reindeer for Christmas, hearts and flowers for Valentine's Day, rabbits and eggs for Easter: those of you who have read my previous books have been around the calendar with me before. So what's left? Well, for starters, here is a whole section full of brand new ideas that *my* kids are currently enjoying: and, kids being kids, I *know* that *your* children will enjoy them too!

2

Lesson 1   The Back-to-School Bus

While not all kids ride back and forth to school by bus, the school bus is a familiar part of the schoolyard scene, and as such it is always a good subject for an art activity.

YOU NEED:

construction paper in the following colors and sizes:
   7½" × 18" yellow
   3" black squares (two each)
   2¼" × 3" white (six each)
paste, pencils, scissors, and crayons

Figure 2-1A

TO PRESENT:

1.   Have your kids draw a square in one of the corners of their yellow paper. (Approximate size: 2½" to 3"). This square is to be cut out and discarded. (See Figure 2-1B.)

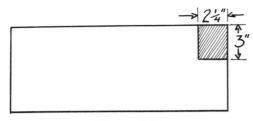

Figure 2-1B

2.   Large circles are then drawn on the black paper and cut out. One of the white papers can be used to draw and cut hub caps. The hub caps are then pasted to the black circles which are in turn pasted onto the school bus to become its wheels.

3.   Have your kids use four of their white papers to draw in the heads and shoulders of some of the passengers. On the last of these white papers do the same for the bus driver. Paste these windows into position, add whatever window trim and lettering is needed, and with *that* you and your kids will have all the buses necessary to bid on next year's transportation contract!

COLUMBUS DAY

One summer when my children were small I took them to Plymouth, Massachusetts to see the replica of the *Mayflower*. While I knew very well that most of them were too young to educationally profit from this adventure, I had substantial hopes that my oldest son had at least reached the age where he could gain some measure of historical enrichment from this kind of a planned experience.

After a long, hot drive to Plymouth, an interminable wait to board the vessel, an extensive tour on deck and below, I grandly shepherded my kids back to the car with that self-satisfied feeling that comes when one instinctively *knows* that he has successfully orchestrated a first-class learning experience.

"Well—any questions?" I asked expansively as I turned the car in the direction of home.

"Yes, Daddy," replied my oldest son. "There is one thing that I still don't understand—what happened to Christopher's other two boats?"

Moral: If you are looking for a can't-fail field trip—try Disneyland.

And if you are looking for a highly successful art lesson, put the emphasis on expressive entertainment and not upon any unrealistic educational expectations!

In *this* spirit, then, I now present you with two of my best Columbus Day lessons:

Lesson 2   'Round the World

"Something new" in a Columbus Day art activity? Try this one. And if you can't use it in October—stick a few Pilgrims on it and launch it in November!

YOU NEED:

5½" × 8½" transparent acetate* (two pieces each)

cellophane tape

construction paper in the following colors and sizes:

   5" × 9" black

   12" × 18" light blue

   1½" × 3½" brown

   2½" square yellow

1⅜" × 12" Measuring Pattern (see Glossary)

pencils, scissors, crayons (and white chalk if white crayons are not available), and paste or glue

TO PRESENT:

1. The two pieces of acetate are joined together with cellophane tape to make a 17" continuous strip of clear

---

*What I use for this lesson are half pieces of the standard 8½" × 11" acetate of the kinds that are used with overhead projectors. If you have an alternate source of acetate supplies in *longer* lengths, please read further into this lesson before cutting your transparent plastic to size.

Figure 2-2A

plastic. I find that the best way to do this is to place both strips against the black construction paper while I butt them together for taping. (The black paper makes the whole operation much more visible.) Any tape extending over the join is then cut off. Since this operation takes a little time, I would suggest that you prepare these strips in advance.

2.   Next we need a Columbus ship appropriate to the skills of your age group. Here is one way I do it:

> *The Hull.* The brown construction paper can be very easily trimmed into a hull shape as shown here in Figure 2-2B. A rudder can be fashioned from one of the cut-away scraps.

> *The Masts.* Once the hull has been taped to the acetate,* the masts and the bow sprit can be drawn on with crayon or permanent fine-line marker.

> *The Sails.* The sails are cut from the yellow paper and the

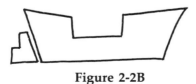

Figure 2-2B

---

*White glue does not adhere satisfactorily to acetate.

red crosses added with crayon. (See Figure 2-2C.) These two are then taped to the transparent plastic.

3. After the ships have been rigged and taped into place, the ends of the acetate are then butted together and taped into a cylinder as shown in Figure 2-2D.

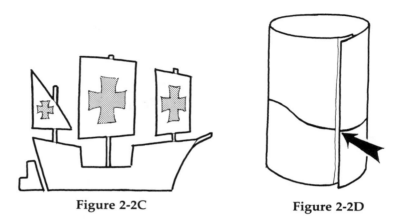

Figure 2-2C   Figure 2-2D

4. Meanwhile your kids can be working on the second part of this activity:

An area the width of the Measuring Pattern is then penciled off at one of the short ends of the 12″ × 18″ light blue construction paper. This area will shortly become the gluing or pasting tab; the remainder of the paper is to become a seascape.

In making this seascape the following suggestions are in order: (1) don't have the gently rolling sea rise much above halfway on the paper and (2) be sure to have the left-hand and the right-hand ends of the sea line prepared so that they will meet when the seascape is formed into a cylinder. (See Figure 2-2D.)

5. Encourage your kids to include an assortment of trans-Atlantic obstacles such as whales, islands, menacing waterspouts, etc.* Use white crayon (or chalk) for clouds, whitecaps, etc.

---

*If your class is still at the age where they see the division between the water and the sky as a water line rather than as a horizon line, forget the obstacles and just draw fish, sunken ships, etc.

6. Once the seascape is finished in crayon, have your kids spread glue on the terminal tab, bring together the opposite ends of the picture, and glue together. The acetate cylinder featuring the Columbus ship under sail is then placed over the seascape.

Slipping this plastic over the paper cylinder is sometimes an object lesson in frustration unless one knows the secret—gently push in one side of the paper cylinder so that it physically takes up less space. Then—simply slip the plastic over the paper cylinder, release the pressure on the latter, and with that the paper cylinder will spring back to its original size.

OPERATING INSTRUCTIONS

As it is normally used, this arcade-like machine sits on the child's desk where it can be activated by holding the acetate stationary with one hand and turning the seascape to the right as indicated in Figure 2-2E. Another way of doing this is to make a handle out of a folded piece of paper and staple in position as shown in Figure 2-2F.

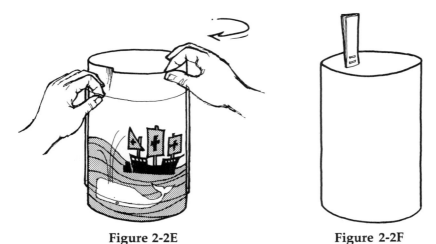

Figure 2-2E   **Figure 2-2F**

Either way these things are fun to operate. With skill and practice these ships can be made to "sail" at great speeds. Much of the fun, of course, comes from learning to navigate these ships in such a way so as not to have them collide with any of the obstacles. (But then—even Columbus must have had his share of troubles here!)

Lesson 3   A Bow for Columbus

Here is as straightforward an approach to a Columbus Day art activity as you will ever find!

YOU NEED:

construction paper
  12″ × 18″ blue
  6″ square brown
  4″ × 12″ blue
  6″ × 9″ yellow
  4½″ × 6″ manila drawing paper
paste, pencils, scissors, and crayons
stapler optional

TO PRESENT:

1.   Invite your kids to make the bow of their caravel by first folding their 6″ square of brown construction paper on the diagonal, and then by rounding the two sides as shown here in Figure 2-3B.

2.   A dab of paste is then placed port and starboard, and the ship is then pasted *low* on the paper in such a way

Figure 2-3A

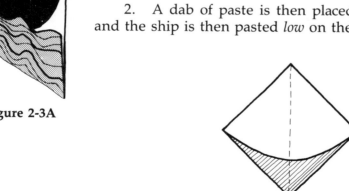

Figure 2-3B

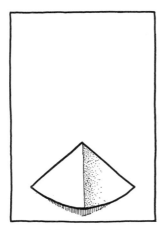

Figure 2-3C

that the bow juts forth in a convincing fashion. (See Figure 2-3C.) (Later, when you have time, you may want to anchor this bow permanently by securing it with a couple of staples.)

Add a tall mast.

3. The 3″ × 12″ blue paper is then trimmed on one of the long sides to represent water, and pasted in place as shown in Figure 2-3A. (Later reinforcing with a couple of staples may also be helpful here.)

4. Have your kids fold their 6″ × 9″ yellow paper in half widthwise and cut on the fold. Paste one of these pieces low on the mast to represent the mainsail. (Figure 2-3D.)

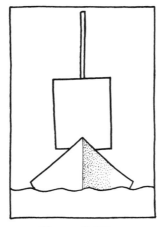

Figure 2-3D

5. Using the yellow remainder from Step 4, fold this paper in half widthwise and cut on the fold. Paste one of these pieces high on the mast to represent the topsail. Between these two sails add the crow's nest! (See Figure 2-3E.)

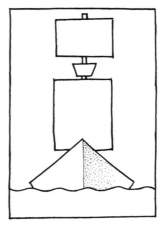

Figure 2-3E

Figure 2-3F

6. The remaining piece of yellow paper can be used to make a cut paper pennant which can be flown from the top of the mast.

7. The manila paper is used to draw and color a crew member (Columbus? A sailor? A child?) See Figure 2-3F. Cut out, cut between arms and body, and perch in the bow as shown in Figure 2-3A.

Sail on!

HALLOWEEN

There are three times in the year when kids are especially supercharged with energy: Christmas, summer recess, and, of course, *Halloween.* The state of excitement that permeates this spooking time is so intense that it is almost impossible to invent a bad Halloween lesson. Given the great material that one has to work with, *good* challenging lessons are always fun to create and a delight to present!

Lesson 4   **Haunted Houses!**

What could be more exciting to a kid at this time of the year than a haunted house? Here are two of the best: the first works beautifully with little children, the second with those just a little bit older.

FIRST ACTIVITY: HAUNTED HOUSES FOR YOUNG SPOOKS

YOU NEED:

12″ × 18″ black construction paper

6″ × 9″ white drawing paper

small scrap of orange construction paper

one single-edged razor blade (or craft knife) and a piece of cardboard to be used as a cutting surface

paste, pencils, scissors, and crayons

Figure 2-4A

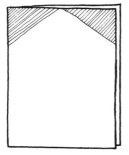

Figure 2-4B

Figure 2-4C

TO PRESENT:

1.   Have your kids fold their black paper in half width-wise, place a dot halfway along one of the short sides and draw two slanting lines as shown in Figure 2-4B.

2.   Cut on these slanted lines through the double layer of paper to make the basic house.

3.   As your kids finish this part of the activity, have them line up so that you can cut out their windows and doors (on the front side only) as suggested in both Figures 2-4A and 2-4C.

4.   Once the windows and doors have been cut out, the house is again refolded and the kids are invited to use their white paper to draw (color if necessary) and cut out "spooks" to inhabit their houses.* The orange paper is for jack-o'-lanterns or anything else your kids want to use it for!

5.   By the time you have recovered from doing all that cutting, you might like to do what I do and that is to invite those kids back who would like to have windows cut in their doors. Since *most* will accept your invitation—this will keep you busy a while longer!

SECOND ACTIVITY: HAUNTED HOUSES FOR OLDER SPOOKS

YOU NEED:

    construction paper in the following colors and sizes:
      two 9" × 12" black
      7" × 12" orange
      6" × 9" white
      4½" × 6" orange
    9" × 11" pattern-weight paperboard
    stapler
    paste, pencils, scissors and crayons

---

*Some children like to keep their spooks free and active, others like to paste them in place. This is an important matter best left up to the spook artists!

Figure 2-4D

PREPARATIONS

Draw the basic house pattern on the pattern-weight paperboard according to the dimensions shown in Figure 2-4E. Cut out the master pattern on the heavy lines and use this master to make a few additional ones so that there will be enough patterns for your kids to share.

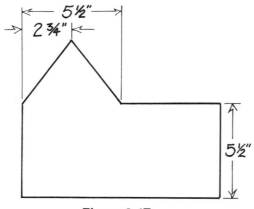

Figure 2-4E

TO PRESENT:

1.   Have your kids trace the house pattern on each of their black papers, and then cut on the heavy lines, cut away the shaded area, and fold on the dotted lines as indicated in Figure 2-4F.

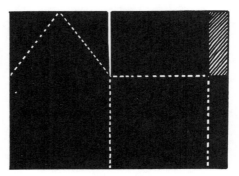

Figure 2-4F

The small rectangular section seen in the lower right of the above figure is a pasting tab which is used to fasten the two parts of the house together as shown in Figure 2-4G.

2.   To save time, staple rather than paste the subroof sections together. (See Figure 2-4H.)

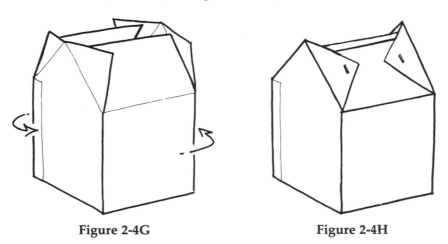

Figure 2-4G   **Figure 2-4H**

3.   Fold the 7″ × 12″ orange paper in half widthwise to make the roof, and simply *place* in position. (Explain to your

kids that since this is only a "play" house, the roof does not need to be pasted or stapled.)

4. The rest of this project is entirely up to your kids. Windows and doors can either be cut out or pasted on. Spooks, pumpkins, etc., can be added inside or out. This activity is limited only by your children's imagination, and at this time of the year, imagination is never in short supply!

Lesson 5 The Door Spider and Other Door Spookers

Since no room needs more than one of these *Door Spookers*, this lesson is not meant to be used as a group activity. Nevertheless—the *Door Spider* is a great classroom entertainer and one the whole class will applaud!

YOU NEED:

> one child or a small committee of children interested in working on an after-school, or other private-time, Halloween project.
>
> nylon fishing line or other strong, lightweight line, thread, or string
>
> assorted scraps as needed (see *Instructions* below.)

Figure 2-5A

INSTRUCTIONS:

Once when I addressed a group of first graders, someone closed the classroom door which in turn startled a huge spider that promptly dropped from the ceiling to dangle its quivering body directly in front of my eyes! The kids greeted my astonishment with great gales of gleeful laughter. The "spider" (of course) was not a spider at all and I was just another duped victim, stalked and caught in a beautifully designed and executed web of a Halloween inspired plan!

Here's how it was done: a large menacing spider has been made from classroom scrap material and fastened onto one end of a length of nylon fishing line. The line had been led through a small ring that had been fastened to the ceiling and then sent across the room to be tied to a small screweye that had been secured high up on the doorknob side of the classroom entry door in such a way that when the door was closed—the spider would make its drop attack! (See Figure 2-5B.)

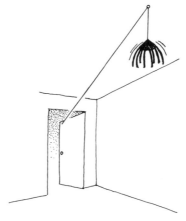

Figure 2-5B

While there are many ways in which to make a respectable spider spooker, here is one quick and easy set of instructions:

1.   Cut out a 5" circle of black construction paper and place dots around its circumference to correspond with the clock face numbers 12 through 8. (See Figure 2-5C.)

2.   Draw a line from the 12 o'clock dot to the middle of the circle and cut on this line. Cut out long spider-like legs from another sheet of black construction paper and attach (paste, glue, staple, or tape) these legs to dots that correspond to the clock face numbers 1-8. (See Figure 2-5D.)

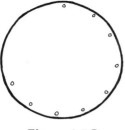

Figure 2-5C

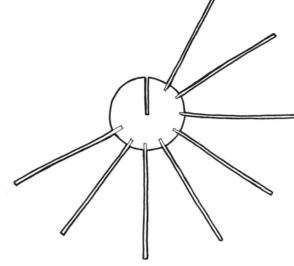

Figure 2-5D

3. *Circlecone** and paste. Add eyes, etc., from scraps of construction paper. Attach to line and prepare your trap! (See Figure 2-5A.)

OTHER SUGGESTIONS:

While spiders are fun, other Halloween creatures can be used as well. Here, in Figure 2-5E, is a good way to make a ghost from a Styrofoam ball and a sheet of white tissue paper. Now, ask your kids what *they* think!

Figure 2-5E

THANKSGIVING

Since history is, by necessity, a matter of selective reporting, it follows that the oft-told tales of the relationship between the Christian Pilgrims and the Heathen Indians may well contain something less than the whole truth. As a matter of fact, the whole history of early New England is

---

*See Glossary.

filled with many great stories that deserve a better audience. Did you know, for example, that:

1.   Samoset, the first Indian to enter the Pilgrim village, greeted the colonists in English and promptly asked for beer?

2.   Some of the Indians who died in the early wars against the white men were former Harvard students?

3.   While the Pilgrims were timidly making their first crossing to the New World, Squanto, who was there to greet them, had already been to England and possibly even to Spain?

Fortunately artists are lousy historians, and while historical art is often amusing, it is never very convincing. So the question here is not "What is historically true?" but rather "What is of importance to children?" The truth is that kids *like* Thanksgiving. They like the costumes, the idea of camping out in the woods; they like the turkey, the cranberry sauce, the pumpkin pie, and—most of all—they like the released time from school.

So don't ruin your Thanksgiving by reading sober history books or by listening to the bitter protest speeches delivered by the Indians who gather at Plymouth each Thanksgiving—instead, celebrate this story for the beautiful fable it is. And if you *must* moralize, talk not of what was but of what might have been.

And save the wishbone for me!

Lesson 6   Pilgrim Starters

Many successful lessons are built on nothing more complicated than artful motivation. When the motivation for this lesson takes the form of Pilgrim hats, you can be sure that the Pilgrims themselves are never far behind!

FIRST ACTIVITY: PILGRIM FATHERS

YOU NEED:

12" × 18" manila drawing paper
4½" × 6" pattern-weight paperboard

construction paper in the following colors and sizes:

4½" × 6" green, brown, blue, or purple

1¼" × 3½" black

1¼" white square

scrap white

(one) pencil compass

paste, pencils, scissors, and crayons

Figure 2-6A

PREPARATION:

Make the master hat pattern according to the following instructions:

1. Draw a line 1¼" from the long edge of the pattern-weight paperboard followed by another 1¼" away from the first as shown in Figure 2-6B.

2. Consult Figure 2-6C. Place the point of the pencil compass in the middle of the uppermost line and draw a 3" arc. The sides of the hat are then drawn 1¾" out from the side of the center of the circle. Cut out the hat shape that is indicated by the dark line. Now—once you have traced this hat pattern and have cut out a few more patterns to share, you are ready to begin!

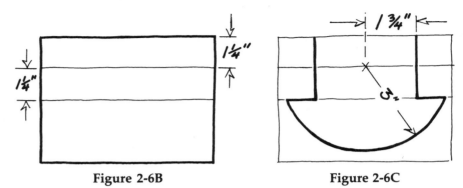

Figure 2-6B

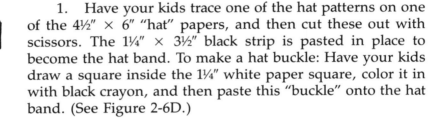

Figure 2-6C

TO PRESENT:

Figure 2-6D

1.   Have your kids trace one of the hat patterns on one of the 4½" × 6" "hat" papers, and then cut these out with scissors. The 1¼" × 3½" black strip is pasted in place to become the hat band. To make a hat buckle: Have your kids draw a square inside the 1¼" white paper square, color it in with black crayon, and then paste this "buckle" onto the hat band. (See Figure 2-6D.)

2.   Fold up the hat brim as shown in Figure 2-6E and then paste the hat band assembly to the main body of the hat, and the hat itself to the top of the manila paper as shown in Figure 2-6A.

Figure 2-6E

3.   The continuation of the Pilgrim picture can be played pretty much by ear, with collar, cuffs, and buckles cut from scraps of white paper. The rest of the picture will take care of itself!

SECOND ACTIVITY: PILGRIM MOTHERS

Whereas most girls will willingly participate in lessons built around Pilgrim men, I can always count on a certain percentage of vocal boys telling me what they think about (ugh!) drawing *girls*. This problem, however, never appears if the subject is not *girls* but *mothers*.

"That's no female; that's my *mom!*"

YOU NEED:

12″ × 18″ manila drawing paper

4½″ × 6″ pattern-weight paperboard construction paper:

    4½″ × 6″ green, blue, brown or purple

    1½″ × 6″ white

    4½″ × 6″ white

(one) pencil compass

paste, pencils, scissors, and crayons

Figure 2-6F

PREPARATIONS:

Make a master hat pattern according to the following instructions:

1. Consult Figure 2-6G. Draw a line 1½″ parallel to one of the long edges of the pattern-weight paperboard. Place the point of your pencil compass in the center of this line and then draw a 2¼″ arc to form the top of Mother's hat. Cut out

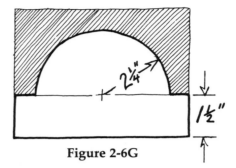

Figure 2-6G

this pattern with scissors, and then trace and cut out a few additional patterns so that you will have enough for your kids to share.

TO PRESENT:

1.   Have your kids trace one of the hat patterns on one of the 4½″ × 6″ "hat" papers, and then cut out these hats with scissors. The bottom part of this hat is then turned up so that the 1½″ × 6″ white strip can be pasted on top. This whole assembly is then pasted to the top of the manila paper (and—if needed—add a dab of paste to the brim to keep it up).

2.   The rest of Mother's picture will develop with little trouble. The collar, cuffs, and apron come from the 4½″ × 6″ white, and the background comes strictly from imagination!

Lesson 7   Log Cabins

The pilgrims did not live in log cabins with solid green roofs. You know this, I know this, and maybe some of your kids know this; but Thanksgiving is no fun at all if one has to be a stickler for detail. Log cabins with solid green roofs are fun to make, and are, in fact, far more practical looking than those drafty and inflammable thatch-topped affairs under which the Pilgrims elected to suffer the cold, damp, and hostile New England winters.

YOU NEED:

construction paper:
   12" × 18" brown (not too dark)
   7" × 10" green
   12" square (or larger) yellow-green
   odds and ends of assorted colors
6" × 9" manila drawing paper
paste, pencils, scissors, and crayons

Figure 2-7A

TO PRESENT:

1.   Using Figure 2-7B as a guide, have your kids fold their 12" × 18" brown paper into 16 parts,* remove the shaded areas, cut on all heavy lines, and position four lightly penciled "X" marks as shown.

2.   Using Figure 2-7C as a guide, draw in the logs. Figure 2-7D is a detail drawing, showing you how the ends of

---

*See *Paper Folding Instructions* in Glossary.

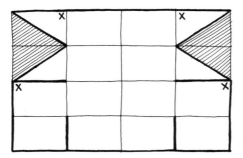

Figure 2-7B

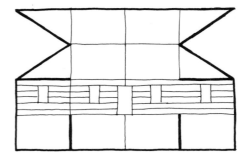

Figure 2-7C

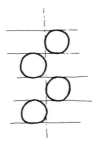

Figure 2-7D

the logs are to be drawn. The doorway and windows are cut out from the manila paper and pasted into place. A door with a paper hinge can be added later if desired. (See Figure 2-7A.)

3. Fold up each house with the top flaps tucked inside in such a way as to bring the X marks into alignment. Paste and add the additional log lines under the peak of the roof when ready. (See Figure 2-7A.)

4. The green roof paper is then folded lengthwise and pasted into position. The house is pasted to the yellow-green "grass."

5. Green paper is then pasted down to make stand-up bushes and the rest of the scene can be left to the kids. They'll have plenty of interesting ideas!

CHRISTMAS

I'll have to confess that I'm still enough of a little boy to enjoy the Pagan excitement of the Christmas season. I like the bells, the decorations, the busy streets, the lights, and festive music. Even the greedy little jingle of the busy cash register is not without its moments of certain nostalgia.

So here in the spirit of Christmas is my gift to you: three of my favorite holiday lessons!

Lesson 8   Christmas in the Country

Once the carcass of the Thanksgiving turkey hits the garbage pail, the Christmas season has begun. This low-key lesson makes the transition with commendable skill!

YOU NEED:

practice paper
12″ × 18″ gray paper
white chalk
pencils and crayons

Figure 2-8A

TO PRESENT:

The near-far concept is often a difficult one for kids to master. This lesson teaches this concept through the artifice of diminishing size and overlapping images.

1. Explain to your class that although there are many ways to draw houses, a lot of kids like to draw them this way:

Figure 2-8B

a. First you draw the front of the house. (See Figure 2-8B.)

b. Then you draw three lines of equal length as shown here in Figure 2-8C.

c. And then you add the other line of the roof and the other end of the house as shown here in Figure 2-8D.

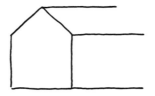 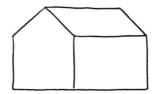

Figure 2-8C   **Figure 2-8D**

2. After your kids have mastered these "two-view" houses on practice paper, review with them the ways in which distance can be achieved through size and position on the picture plane. (See Figure 2-8E.)

3. When this is understood, show them how this illusion of depth can be nailed down through the use of overlapping images. (See Figure 2-8F.)

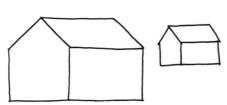 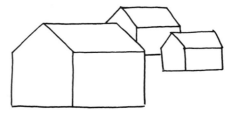

Figure 2-8E   **Figure 2-8F**

4. When your short period of instruction is over, pass out your materials and let your kids get to work. The chalk, of course, is for the snow!

Lesson 9   A Time for Reflection

Here's a Christmas art activity with a brand new look!

YOU NEED:

> construction paper in the following colors and sizes:
>> 12" × 18" pastel
>>
>> 9" red square
>>
>> 2" × 11" brown
>>
>> 2¼" × 3" red
>>
>> assorted scraps as needed
>
> 5" × 8" lightweight paperboard
>
> 6" × 9" kitchen foil*
>
> paste, pencils, scissors, and crayons

Figure 2-9A

TO PRESENT:

1. Have your kids cut a square out of one side of the red paper to make a fireplace. Draw in the bricks. (See Figure

---

*Buy the 12" rolls and with the help of a paper cutter this preliminary cut-up job is not as onerous as it sounds!

2-9B.) The 2″ × 11″ brown paper is then folded lengthwise
and the lower half pasted to the back of the fireplace to make
a mantel. (Trim off that part of the brown that shows from the
front. Paste the total assembly to the lower half of the 12″ ×
18″ pastel paper as shown in Figure 2-9A.)

Figure 2-9B

2.   When passing out the foil, do so with the "good"
(shiniest) side down. Have your kids place their 5″ × 8″
paperboard rectangles squarely on top and then fold the
protruding foil over this paperboard "mirror backing." Add
paste to the backing and paste to the "wall" above the
mantle.

3.   From here on in this activity can be pretty much
played by ear. For those who need instructions in stocking
making, the small red paper with a corner rectangle removed
is as good a way to begin as any. (See Figure 2-9C.)

Figure 2-9C

4.   A blazing fire, a candle or two on the mantle,
packages on the floor . . . your kids will think of many ways
to make this nostalgic scene a favorite for all ages.

Lesson 10   The Best of the Lot

Some lessons are just naturally showier than others.
This is one of those lessons!

YOU NEED:

9″ × 12″ pattern-weight paperboard
construction paper:

12" × 18" green

small scraps of assorted colors as needed

8½" × 11" lightweight paper (duplicating or mimeo supplies work well here)

scrap paper

paper punch

paste, pencils, scissors, and crayons

Figure 2-10A

PREPARATIONS:

Consult the Glossary for instructions in making a *Perfect Sailboat Cone.** Make this Sailboat Cone from a sheet of the 12" × 18" green construction paper, and with this flattened cone as your guide, make as many cone-making patterns as will be needed for classroom sharing. (See Figure 2-10B.)

Figure 2-10B

---

*See *Sailboat Cone* in Glossary.

Also make a number of 8¼" circle patterns from your paperboard stock.

Now you are ready to begin!

TO PRESENT:

1.   With the help of the cone-making patterns have your kids construct Perfect Sailboat Cones from their 12" × 18" paper.

2.   Trace the circle pattern on the 8½" × 11" paper and cut out this circle. The cut-out circle is then folded in half and folded in half again as shown in Figures 2-10C and 2-10D. Then, using Figure 2-10E as a guide, have your kids draw lines like those indicated.

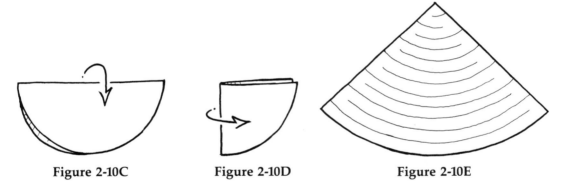

Figure 2-10C   **Figure 2-10D**   **Figure 2-10E**

3.   Once these lines have been cut with scissors, have your kids snip off a little bit at the top and then carefully unfold this packet. The resulting paper will look something like that shown here in Figure 2-10F.

4.   Have your kids shove a small ball of scrap paper up inside the cone to fill it out and to allow it to stand solidly on flat surfaces. Slip the circular paper over the top of this cone and carefully pull it down until it looks something like that shown in Figure 2-10A. Paste the ends so that this decoration will stay put.

5.   Now pass out small scraps of colored paper and invite your kids to decorate their trees. If you have time, wander through their midst with a pad of assorted papers

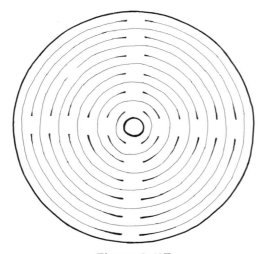

Figure 2-10F

and paper punch small handfuls of dots for your kid to use as they see fit.

Merry Christmas!

NEW YEAR'S

Like many teachers, I have spent large segments of my life working at jobs that have been about as remote from teaching as Peking is from Peoria. And New Year's? I have spent nearly every New Year's of my adult life in some crepe-paper festooned restaurant or cocktail lounge playing piano for revelers ("Hey, Buddy, can you play 'My Melon Call Me Baby'?") while my truant mind wandered elsewhere. New Year's may or may not be for celebrating, but it is hardly the best time of the year for lesson plans!

When kids return to school on January 2nd, the party's over; the New Year's celebration is already as cold as yesterday's mashed potatoes. At this late date, kids can take a warmed-up New Year's lesson or they can leave it. So what's a poor teacher to do? Salute the New Year—or forget it?

What do *I* do? Some years I give a New Year's lesson, some years I don't. It depends. But when I do, I often return to an old favorite of mine that I call the *Great Baby Mystery.* Read it through and I think you'll immediately see why I like it!

Lesson 11   The Great Baby Mystery

Why does a baby look like a baby? As your kids are soon to discover, this question is *not* as stupid as it sounds!

PREPARATION:

Make a copy of Figure 2-11A and 2-11B, cut them out and paste them on white paper. Fold the baby silhouette where indicated and then unfold. *Now* you are ready to begin.

YOU NEED:

construction paper:
    9" × 12" assorted flesh colors
    9" × 12" assorted darks
    3" × 4½" white
    odds and ends of other assorted colors
two prepared silhouettes (see above)
3½" (water cup size) circle pattern
paste, pencil, scissors, and crayons

PRELIMINARY CLASSROOM DISCUSSION:

Show your silhouettes to your class, one picture at a time. Once your kids have seen both, ask them what they saw (a man and a child). Then comes the big question: "Why did you call one a man and the other a child?"

"Because one *looked* like a man and the other like a child."

"We *know* that one looked like a man and the other looked like a child. What we want to know is *why*"

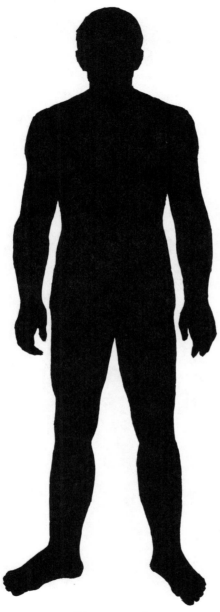

Figure 2-11A

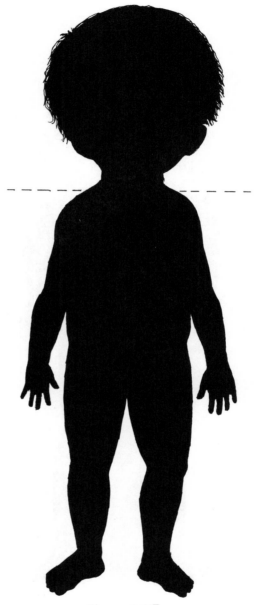

Figure 2-11B

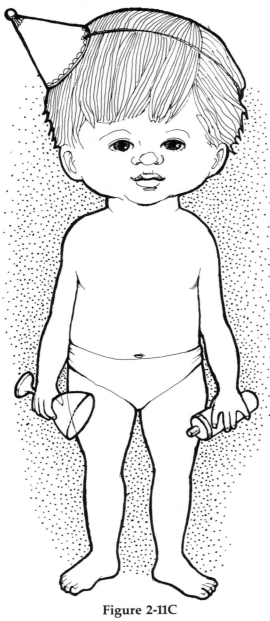

Figure 2-11C

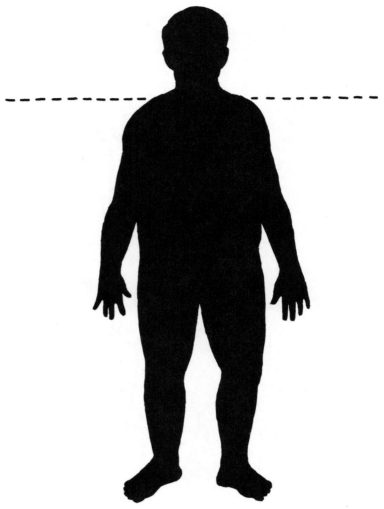

Figure 2-11D

"Because the man has muscles and the baby doesn't?"

"So what—I have seen a lot of strong babies and some pretty flabby men!"

"Because the baby was fat and the man wasn't?"

Same kind of answer as before. "I have seen a lot of fat men and some pretty skinny babies. So that can't be the answer either!"

"Because the man is taller than the child?"

"Wrong again! They are both the same size!" (Briefly hold up the silhouettes side by side to prove your point.)

After much laughter and scratching of heads, someone inevitably arrives at the correct observation that the baby's head is larger in relationship to the rest of its body than the man's. Nail this point down by folding the baby's head back on the prefolded line and placing it over the adult silhouette so that the kids can see what a man's head would look like on a child's body! (See Figure 2-11D.)

Now the art lesson can begin!

TO PRESENT:

1. Have your kids lightly trace the circle pattern with their pencils three times as shown in Figure 2-11E. Explain to your kids that when drawing people, many artists think not in terms of feet and inches (or meters and millimeters) but in *heads*. By this the artist is referring to the relationship of the head to the rest of the body. For example: while the silhouette of the man may be 7½ or 8 *heads* high, for this baby lesson three tangent circles will do the job.*

2. After the face is drawn in have your kids sketch in the rest of the body using the circles *not as outline suggestions* but only as proportional guides. (See Figure 2-11F.)

3. Cut out the finished baby.

4. In my presentation I generally choose this point in

Figure 2-11E

Figure 2-11F

---

*While a baby three heads high may be an outrageous exaggeration of a normal baby's head to body ratio, a three-circle baby is relatively easy to learn. And compared to, say, the head-body ratio of Charlie Brown of *Peanuts* fame, this body is reasonably well-proportioned! (Charlie Brown is approximately 2¼ heads high.)

my lesson to become quite obviously flustered. I mutter a few worried "oh-oh's" to myself as I scurry around trying to locate the small pieces of white paper which I then quickly pass out to each of the kids. It's diaper paper, and I let it be known that since I don't want any "accidents," I want them to get their diapers on their babies as soon as possible!*

To make the diapers fit the baby, simply have your kids place their babies on the diapers and trace the necessary dimensions directly from the body; remove the figure to add the missing lines, cut out and paste to baby. (See Figures 2-11G and 2-11H.)

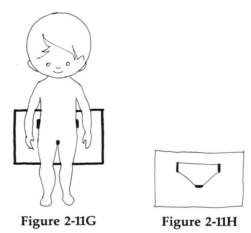

Figure 2-11G   **Figure 2-11H**

5.   Once the baby is diapered, paste the baby to the darker paper and add whatever decorations may be needed! (See Figure 2-11C.)

THE PRESIDENTIAL HOLIDAYS

It's too bad that we don't do more with our Presidents' birthdays; you know, like exchanging cherry pies on Washington's, wire taps on Nixon's, etc. It could be lots of fun. In the meantime, however, let's continue concentrating our

---

*Of course this comedy interlude is "childish," it's supposed to be! I teach kids, not Broadway critics. While a bit of business like this diaper routine will definitely not get you a booking on the late-night talk shows, it *always* gets a good classroom reception. And *that's* what counts!

festive efforts on the Two Big Ones: Washington's and Lincoln's:

Lesson 12 How to Draw George Washington Hats (et cetera)

While pure, unbridled, and untutored forms of self-expression are often fun to do and beautiful to behold, they are also totally unreliable means of communication. If you believe otherwise, prove it by drawing for me a convincing George Washington-style, three-cornered hat....

And if *you* can't draw one and *your* kids can't draw one, I say, "To hell with the proponents of 100% free expression!" *Here's* how:

YOU NEED:

pencils
practice paper
drawing paper and crayons (or other art media)

Figure 2-12A

GEORGE WASHINGTON HATS

Figure 2-12B

1. If you can teach your kids to draw a "V," you're well on your way to teaching them how to make a pretty fair George Washington hat. (See Figures 2-12B through 2-12E.)

2. Now add George Washington. (See Figure 2-12F.)

Figure 2-12C

Figure 2-12D

Figure 2-12E

Figure 2-12F

DRAWING THE ET CETERA

And now that we have his hat on, we can either let this famous man wear grungy contemporary clothes or take this opportunity to teach our kids a little history via the plumage of yesteryear's fashions.

1. Have your kids lightly pencil in the basic human body as indicated in Figure 2-12G.

2. Since we already know how to make the hat, let's begin now with the coat. (See Figure 2-12H.) Add a little lace at the cuffs.

3. After the coat come the vest, the ruffled shirt, and the knee britches. (See Figure 2-12I.)

4. And finally, add the long stockings and the buckled shoes as suggested in Figure 2-12A.

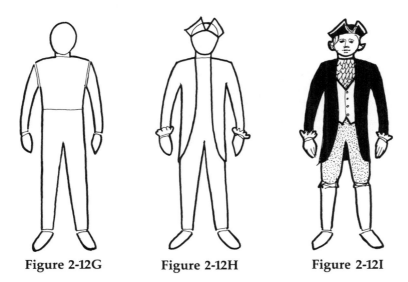

Figure 2-12G   Figure 2-12H   Figure 2-12I

CONCLUDING ACTIVITY:

After your kids have experimented with Colonial costuming and have heard you spin a few tales about Ol' George, hand out the drawing paper and the art supplies, and let them do it *their* way!

Lesson 13   Stand Up for Lincoln!

In many ways Lincoln's Birthday is a celebration of the cylinder. His much-publicized cabin was made with cylindrical logs, his tall stovepipe hat was another famous cylinder, and now, thanks to this lesson, we learn that only a cylindrical head could have fit into his cylindrical hat! In any case, here is a Lincoln that can stand up among the best of them!

YOU NEED:

9″ × 12″ manila drawing paper

black construction paper in the following sizes:

4½″ × 12″

6″ square

Figure 2-13A

2″ × 12″

3½″ (water cup size) circle pattern

9″ × 12″ pattern prepared as shown in Figure 2-13B

paste, pencils, scissors, and crayons

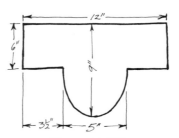

Figure 2-13B

TO PRESENT:

1. Have your kids paste the 4½″ × 12″ black to the manila paper as shown in Figure 2-13C.

Figure 2-13C

2.   To make the hat brim, begin by having the circle traced to the middle of the black square. A dot is then placed in the middle of this circle and spoke-like lines are drawn in. (See Figure 2-13D.) The outer circle is drawn freehand. The kids are then instructed to cut on the outer circle and, after poking a hole in the center "hub," to cut on each "spoke" line.

3.   Returning now to the paper prepared in Step 1, place the paperboard pattern on top of the Step 1 assembly and lightly trace the curved portion. Using this lightly penciled area as the limits to Old Abe's face, have your kids draw in his beard as shown in Figure 2-13E. Large ears are then added to each side of the beard, and the face is drawn in.

Figure 2-13D

Figure 2-13E

4.   Once the front of the head is complete, it is time for a trial assemblage of the component parts. The head is rolled up into a loose cylinder and the hat brim is slipped on over the head. Now that your kids get the general idea, it will be easy for them to visualize where the collar, coat, and back of the hair should be positioned. (See Figure 2-13F.*)

---

*Needless to say, no child's drawing is going to end up looking like the illustrations on this or any other page in this book. Nor should they. (On the other hand, while I have no intentions of falsifying any of my drawings so they will pass as work done by a child—some of them are not too far removed!)

Figure 2-13F

5.   When ready for assembling, the only thing left to do is to add on the 2″ × 12″ hat band which will not only hide the "spokes" of the hat brim but add a needed note of fashion as well!

ST. VALENTINE'S DAY

In order to stamp out the fervor of traditional paganism and to harness some of this ancient energy into the service of Christ, the early Christian church often resorted to that old ecclesiastical trick of pretending to join into traditional celebrations when it was, in fact, deliberately and diligently doing its best to replace these pagan festivities with holy days. St. Valentine (bless his soul) may very well have been martyred by the Romans on February 14th, but the lusty roots of this heart-shaped celebration gain strength, not from the life of a dimly remembered saint, but from the pagan vitality of the February *15th* lovers' feast of the ancient Roman Lupercalia. Now—take a good look at Valentine's Day. Reflect on what it means to your kids. And then take a good look at yourself in the mirror.

I think the pagans won. Long live the Lupercalia!

Lesson 14   An Old-Fashioned Valentine

Valentines come in many flavors. While this *Old-Fashioned Valentine* is new, it is as traditional in spirit as red hearts and white lace!

YOU NEED:

9" × 12" white drawing paper
9" × 12" red construction paper
scraps of red and white paper
paste, scissors, and crayons

Figure 2-14A

TO PRESENT:

1.   Have your kids fold their 9" × 12" papers in half widthwise. Then have them set their white papers to one side while they go to work on the red.

The front cover of the red paper is to be folded in about 1½" (or less) from the open side as shown here in Figure

2-14B. (Exact dimensions unimportant.) Use this folded edge to cut a piece—skip a piece, "snowflake" style, as suggested here in Figure 2-14C.

2.   Set aside the red paper and begin now with the white. Fold the white paper on the fold side as shown in Figure 2-14D. Then exercise this fold back and forth until it loses its directional memory. Cut decorative pieces from this center fold as suggested in Figure 2-14E, and then reverse this center fold as shown in Figure 2-14F.

3.   The remainder of this lesson is best Quarterbacked.* Apply paste to the inside of the red cover at the outside edge, and press the folded white paper into position as shown in Figure 2-14G. Lift up the right-hand edge of this white packet to slip a little paste under it to completely adhere the downside surface to the red construction paper.

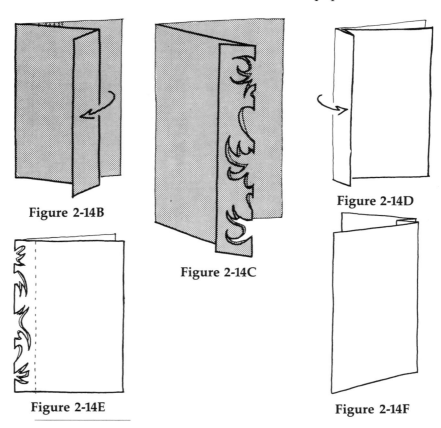

Figure 2-14B

Figure 2-14C

Figure 2-14D

Figure 2-14E

Figure 2-14F

*See Glossary for *Quarterbacking*.

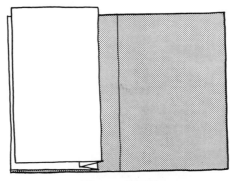

Figure 2-14G

4. Add paste to the top surface of the white packet. Fold over the right-hand side of the red card as you would close a book, and press again.

Open at once and the valentine is now ready for added embellishments. Encourage your kids to use the scraps of red and white to add additional decorations inside and out.

Happy Valentine's Day!

Lesson 15   A Valentine Pick-Me-Up

Here's a novel way to add a new dimension to your Valentine celebrations:

YOU NEED:

white drawing paper 8″ and 9″ square

red construction paper:

9″ × 18″

9″ square

paste, pencils, scissors, and crayons

TO PRESENT:

1. Have your kids fold their 9″ × 18″ red paper widthwise and set aside for later.

2. The 8″ square of white is folded into quarters and using the cut-a-piece—skip-a-piece "snowflake" approach, is

Figure 2-15A

quickly and efficiently transformed into a decorative lace-like cover decoration. Paste in place on the folded red construction paper. (See Figure 2-15B.)

3.   The 9″ square of white is pasted inside the card as shown in Figure 2-15C.

Figure 2-15B

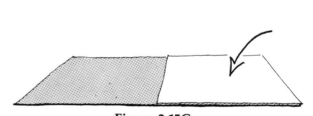

Figure 2-15C

4.   The 9″ red is folded in half and a large half-heart is penciled in against the fold as shown here in Figure 2-15D. This line is then cut through both parts of the folded paper to create a large folded heart.

Figure 2-15D

5.   Now comes the hard part. Lines must be drawn onto this folded heart in the manner indicated in Figure 2-15E. Cut on these lines.

6.   A small "PICK-ME-UP" tab is then pasted to the center of this heart as shown in Figure 2-15F.

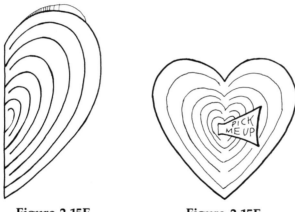

Figure 2-15E   **Figure 2-15F**

7.   A short message or greeting is written on the center of the inside white paper that was pasted in position in Step 3. The *outside edge* (only!) is then pasted onto this same white background in such a way as to completely hide the secret words.

And that's it: a valentine with a "Pick-Me-Up" message all loaded and waiting to explode!

ST. LEPRECHAUN'S DAY

In recent years there has been a revival of popular interest in the Little People and consequently the Hobbits, Gnomes, Fairies, Dwarfs, Elves, Orcs and Half-Orcs have never enjoyed a better press—which all goes to prove what the kids knew all along: This kind of stuff is *fun!*

Lesson 16   An Irish Trick

Add animation to an art project and you'll invariably have the makings of a sure-fire winner. Add this pop-up Leprechaun to your list of St. Patrick's Day activities and you'll also have the classroom means to slip in a painless lesson on basic human proportions!

YOU NEED:

9" × 12" green construction paper
9" × 12" drawing paper
paste, pencils, scissors, and crayons

Figure 2-16A

TO PRESENT:

1. Have your kids fold their drawing paper in half lengthwise and then slightly off-center widthwise. Position as shown in Figure 2-16B.

2. Draw a line from the intersection of the two folds to the bottom of the paper to establish the line that will divide the legs and feet. (See dark line on Figure 2-16C.)

3. Whatever the character of the Leprechaun it must be drawn centered on the fold as shown in Figure 2-16D. Note also the following:

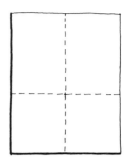

Figure 2-16B

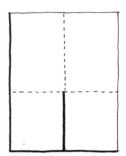

Figure 2-16C

Figure 2-16D

   the abnormally large head which is so typical of many of the Little People.

   the placement of the wrists which even on all normally proportioned people fall on a line opposite the beginning of the legs. Furthermore it is essential to the Pop-Up mechanism that the wrists fall on this line.

   the feet: which must be drawn as if the Leprechaun is standing on tiptoes.

4.   The 9″ × 12″ green construction paper is then folded in half widthwise and the cut-out Leprechaun is positioned (but *not* pasted!) straddling the center fold towards the top of the green paper. Now—paste only one leg and one hand from the same side of the body to the green paper. (Do not paste the *foot.*) Then fold up the body on top of the one pasted leg and hand as shown in Figures 2-16E, 2-16F, and 2-16G.

Figure 2-16E

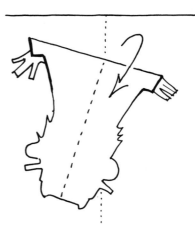

Figure 2-16F

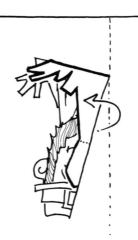

Figure 2-16G

5. When this accordion-like fold is complete, have your kids apply paste to the back of the other leg and hand, and then carefully close the cover of the card to make contact with the pasted surface. Press—then open! Happy St. Patrick's Day!

ADDITIONAL SUGGESTIONS:

If the Leprechaun needs a bag of gold, this can be done using the same Pop-Up principle. (See Figures 2-16H.) The pasting tabs are then covered with small strips of green paper to hide them.

Rather than pasting the hands, one or both can be freed as shown in Figure 2-16A. Simply fold the arm (or arms) at the elbow and let it do its own thing!

Figure 2-16H

Lesson 17 Leprechauns on the Side

While it is possible to teach kids the difference between front view, side view, and back view, the whole concept of *views* is educationally sterile unless, of course, these views are of something of *real* interest to your learners.

Like *Leprechauns*!

YOU NEED:

practice paper

6″ × 12″ white drawing paper and small scraps of same construction paper

  6″ × 12″ yellow-green

  4½″ × 6″ green

paste, pencils, scissors, and crayons

PRELIMINARY PRACTICE:

Have your kids use their practice paper and pencils to follow you as you present the following concepts on the chalkboard:

Figure 2-17A

Figure 2-17B

Figure 2-17C

Figure 2-17D

1.   Lightly draw a profile something like the one shown here in Figure 2-17B. (Large noses encouraged!)

2.   Then proceed to show your kids the way in which hair would grow on the side of a bald, chin-whiskered Leprechaun. (See Figures 2-17C and 2-17D.)

Once your kids have reached the point where they get the idea, you are ready to present the main event:

TO PRESENT:

1.   Have your kids draw a large, profile of a bald-headed, chin-whiskered Leprechaun at the top of their 6″ × 12″ white drawing paper. Once this head has been drawn, the side view figure can follow. (Review the full-length side view concept as needed.)

2.   Since kids work at different speeds, your best bet is

to wait until everyone is at least through with the drawing of the head before announcing: "I know that many of you are far from being finished, but *now* is as good a time as any to explain the next step. Will everyone—done or not—please draw a line from the forehead off to one side of the paper, and from the back of the bald part of the head to the other side of the paper."

Once they have followed these instructions, have your kids *Scribble-Cancel** the top as shown in Figure 2-17E, and then cut away this section.

Figure 2-17E

3. With the Scribble-Canceled area cleared away, invite your kids to place their 4½" × 6" green paper behind their Lephrechaun's head to lightly pencil in two vertical lines: the first from the forehead up, the second from the back of the head up as shown in Figure 2-17F.

Figure 2-17F

*See Glossary.

4.   Remove the top paper, connect the two lines on the green paper with a curved line on top and with an ellipse below. (See Figure 2-17G.) Then draw a second ellipse around the first ellipse and erase the lines indicated by dashes in Figure 2-17H. The Leprechaun's basic hat is now nearly complete.

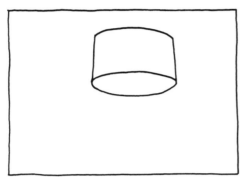
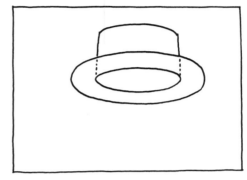

Figure 2-17G   **Figure 2-17H**

5.   Darken the outline of the hat with a black crayon before cutting it out. Add the seen portion of the hat band, and cut out and paste down the part of the buckle that would be seen from this viewpoint. Use a piece of scrap white paper for this last operation. (See Figure 2-17I.)

Figure 2-17I

6.   With the help of a Paper-Poker,* have your kids punch a hole into the hat's inside oval (shaded section: Figure 2-17I) before removing same with scissors. The hat with its now empty interior can be placed on the Leprechaun's head at any preferred angle and pasted in place now or later.

7.   Once the full figure has been colored in and cut out,

_____

*See Glossary.

have your kids paste the completed assembly to their yellow-green paper and display! (See Figure 2-17A.)

EASTER

Although I have been the teacher of thousands and the father of four, never once has any child ever asked me to explain what relationship, if any, the funny-looking, two-legged, egg-painting, basket-toting rabbits had with the resurrection of Christ.

Perhaps it is just as well!

Lesson 18   An Easter Bag Basket

While I have yet to invent an Easter bag made out of a basket, here is an Easter basket made out of a bag!

YOU NEED:

construction paper:
  6″ × 9″ green
  assorted scraps
flat-bottomed lunch bags
stapler
pencils, scissors, and crayons

Figure 2-18A

TO PRESENT:

1.   Have your kids lay their bags down on their desks with the bottom flap up, and invite them to feel the ridges indicated by the dotted lines in Figure 2-18B.

2.   Once these inside-fold ridges are identified, pencil in both ridge lines. Have your kids *Scribble-Cancel** the areas

---

*See Glossary.

Figure 2-18B

Figure 2-18C

as indicated by shading in Figure 2-18C. These areas are then cut away.

3. Once the shaded areas have been removed, open each bag to staple the two long strips together to make a handle. (See Figure 2-18A.)

4. Finally, cut the green paper into long strips; these strips are then crumbled and placed in the basket as grass-like excelsior. Use the odds and ends of colored paper for making eggs, etc. (And, if possible, drop in a few little candy tidbits of your own.)

Happy Easter!

Lesson 19   Putting Your Eggs in One Basket

Here's a very serviceable basket. If you can't find time to use it for Easter you can always save the lesson, substitute fruit or vegetables for eggs, and present it anytime!

YOU NEED:

    construction paper: assorted Easter colors in the follow-
      ing sizes:

      9″ × 12″ background paper

      6″ × 9″ basket paper with matching 1⅛″ × 9″ handle

      2¼″ × 12″ table paper

      3″ × 4½″ egg papers (including white)

      4½″ × 6″ chocolate egg or bunny paper (optional)

    (one) 2″ × 9″ drawing paper

    2″ × 9″ pattern-weight paperboard

    paste, pencils, scissors, and crayons

PREPARATION:

Using the 2″ × 9″ drawing paper, prepare an ellipse that is approximately the same size as the drawing paper. Here's one good way:

Figure 2-19A

1. Fold the 2″ × 9″ drawing paper into quarters as shown in Figures 2-19B and 2-19C.

2. Trim off the shaded portions shown in Figure 2-19D. Open up. If the ellipse is not the way you want it, refold and trim until it comes out right! (See Figure 2-19E.)

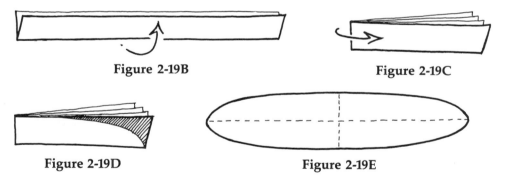

Figure 2-19B

Figure 2-19C

Figure 2-19D

Figure 2-19E

3. Trace this ellipse onto the 2″ × 9″ pattern-weight paperboard. Cut out this new sturdy master pattern and use it to trace out enough ellipses for your class to share.

TO PRESENT:

1. Explain to your kids that many artists use the ellipse idea for drawing things like bowls, cups, etc. Using Figures

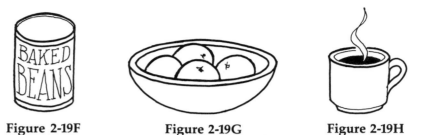

Figure 2-19F   **Figure 2-19G**   **Figure 2-19H**

2-19F, 2-19G, and 2-19H as your guide, use the chalkboard or selected pictures to make your point.

2.   Then pass out the ellipse patterns and have your kids trace them onto their 6″ × 9″ basket paper (with an added "T" for "top") as shown here in Figure 2-19I. Then, draw in the bottom of the basket as suggested here in Figure 2-19J.

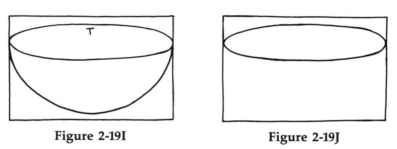

Figure 2-19I   **Figure 2-19J**

3.   Once this part of the basket has been drawn and cut out, have your kids *Scribble-Cancel** the back. When the Scribble-Canceling is complete, it is time to separate the ellipse from the base of the basket. (See Figure 2-19K.)

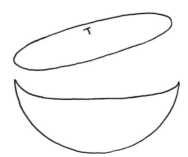

Figure 2-19K

*See Glossary.

4. The table paper is then pasted to the bottom of the background paper, and *the curved outside edge (only) of the basket is pasted in place in such a way as to create a usable pocket.* The ellipse is then pasted into position.

5. Now—before the paste on the ellipse has had a chance to dry, slip one end of the handle paper under this ellipse as shown in Figure 2-19L. Note in this figure how the handle is inserted at a slight angle and is positioned slightly off center.

6. Place a small amount of paste on the other end of the handle and bend it over to paste against the inside of the basket paper as shown in Figure 2-19M. And with that—your basic basket is complete!

Figure 2-19L

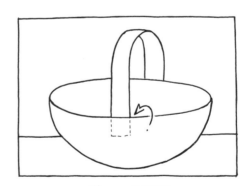

Figure 2-19M

EGG DECORATING INSTRUCTIONS

While your kids may be perfectly satisfied coloring and decorating their eggs without any suggestions from you at all, the following ideas might also be put to good use:

How to Make Parallel Decorations

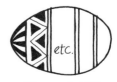

Figure 2-19N

Simply draw parallel lines on the cut paper eggs and decorate with repeat patterns as suggested in Figure 2-19N.

Figure 2-19O

How To Make Form-Fitting Decorations

Have your kids begin at one end of the egg with a small circle and continue outward with concentric circles or parts of circles as shown in Figure 2-19O. And then decorate to taste!

And that's that. Encourage your kids to make all kinds of eggs, candy, and even chocolate rabbits that can be cut out and placed in the pockets of their baskets. Bows, basket decorations, etc., can be added as desired! (See Figure 2-19A.)

WHEN IT'S TIME TO SALUTE THE COLORS

There are a number of occasions in the school year when flag lessons can be put to very good use: Veteran's Day and Memorial Day being the first two that come to mind. On the other hand—since kids like flags and flag lessons—any time at all is a good time to invite your kids to rally around the flag!

Lesson 20   Sticking with Your Country's Flag

To judge by the number of elementary papers that kids bring home from school decorated with colorful gummed stickers, stickers continue to be a popular as well as a reasonably inexpensive form of classroom reward. Teachers can always find uses for them, kids never seem to tire of them, and whenever I get my hands on some, I can generally find a way to work them into a rewarding art activity!

Figure 2-20A

YOU NEED:

flag stickers
drawing paper
crayons (or other art materials)

TO PRESENT:

Simply discuss with your class the many ways in which a flag (or flags) could be used in a picture (parades, patriotic holidays, scout camps, boats and ships, etc.). Then—pass out the paper and sticker(s) and invite your kids to create their own flag pictures.

Lesson 21   A Preruled Flag

While the sticker flag of the previous lesson has its uses, it also places built-in limits to the size of the accompanying picture. For larger pictures you might need a larger flag—and nothing could be easier to make than a (considerably larger) *Preruled Flag*!

YOU NEED:

> sheet of lined white paper
> small scrap of blue construction paper
> 12" × 18" drawing paper
> white chalk
> paste, pencils, scissors, and crayons

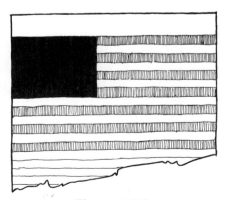

Figure 2-21A

TO PRESENT:

1.   Explain to your class that the American flag has thirteen stripes, and that the first and the thirteenth stripes are red. Then pass out the lined white paper and invite your kids to use these lines to lay out the basic flag. (See Figure 2-21A.)

2.   Since the thirteen stripes will not use up all of the lined paper, trim off the unused portion.

3.   After the flag is colored and cut out, the blue field of colored construction paper is pasted in one corner of the flag in such a way as to cover the top seven stripes (four red and three white). The chalked stars can be added once the blue field is in position.

4.   And that's it! Simply have your kids paste their flags to their drawing paper and begin.

They'll know what to do!

MOTHERS, FATHERS, ETC.

Some of us can still remember the time when a teacher could give a Mother's Day or Father's Day classroom lesson without preface. Divorces were rare, unmarried mothers even rarer, and unmarried couples living together were almost unheard of. Today divorce is common, unmarried mothers abound, and trying to figure out the living arrangements between divorced couples with children is sometimes about as confusing to follow as a quick game of seven-card stud, jacks and queens wild. Social changes I can understand; but when this social change hurts children, *that* grieves me.

I doubt if anyone, except those who have been conscientious parents themselves, has any real understanding of the amount of love, worry, time, energy, sacrifice, and hard-earned money that goes into conscientious parenting. Those of us who come from relatively stable homes—what do we know of the anguish, the problems, and the silent pain that must go into and accompany single-parent child raising? What toll do these homes take from children and what singular sacrifices must be performed by the one parent who is forced into playing the role of two people? And what of the children who come from foster homes, or from the wide spectrum of troubled homes in which strife and hostility are normalcy?

If there was ever a time when parents or their surrogates need all the honoring they can get—it is now. Mother's Day and Father's Day are no longer reserved just for blood parents, it is a day to give full and loving recognition to *all* the people who have been strong enough to accept the heavy burdens of the actual *parenting*.

So if my advice is worth anything here, it is this: Don't cripple your effectiveness as a teacher by exclusively refer-ring to these cards as Mother's Day or Father's Day cards; they should be thought of as male and female parenting cards, and, as such, your children should be freely encour-aged to give these gifts of love to any person they wish to honor.

They'll know *who* and how many—and *that's* what's important here!

Lesson 22   Flowers for the Mother in Your Life

If you are looking for a bright and attractive greeting card, look no further—this one's for *you!*

YOU NEED:

construction paper:
3" × 4½", 5" × 8" and 9" × 12" white
5½" × 8" pink
flower-colored and leaf-colored scraps
practice paper
paste, pencils, scissors, and crayons

TO PRESENT:

1.   Have your kids practice the following table-making

Figure 2-22A

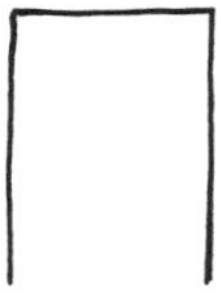

Figure 2-22B

Figure 2-22C

Figure 2-22D

schema on a piece of scrap paper. (See Figures 2-22B, 2-22C, and 2-22D.)

    2.   Once your kids get the idea, have them draw a "good" table on the 5" × 8" paper positioned something like the one pictured in Figure 2-22E. The floor line and the colored wall are extras.

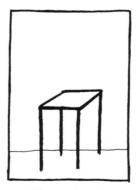

Figure 2-22E

3. Beginning with an oval, have your kids use the smallest white paper to draw and decorate a vase. Then cut it out and paste it to the top of the table. (See Figures 2-22F and 2-22A.)

4. From the top of this vase, stem lines should be crayoned in as shown in Figure 2-22G and the scraps of flower-colored paper used to make cut and torn paper flowers that can then be pasted into place.

Figure 2-22F

5. The leaves are made from scraps of green paper. A most effective way of presenting the leaves is to paste them only at the bottom so that they can either flare out or curl out at the top in a realistic fashion.

6. The card is easily finished. The picture is mounted on the 5½″ × 8½″ pink paper which is, in turn, mounted on the front cover of the widthwise folded 9″ × 12″ white paper.

7. And that's it. If there is any finishing to do—your kids will do it themselves!

Lesson 23   A Famous Man-About-Town Card and Envelope

Figure 2-22G

As the greeting card industry learned a long time ago, *everyone* likes surprises!

YOU NEED:

6″ × 18″ and 2″ × 4″ white drawing paper

6″ × 12″ pastel-colored construction paper

1″ × 18″ strips of construction paper "ribbon"

paste, pencils, scissors, and crayons

TO PRESENT:

THE BASIC CARD

1. Have your kids place their 6″ × 12″ paper on top of the 6″ × 18″ paper and use it as a pattern to make the first fold. (See Figure 2-23B.) Remove this pattern and fold the

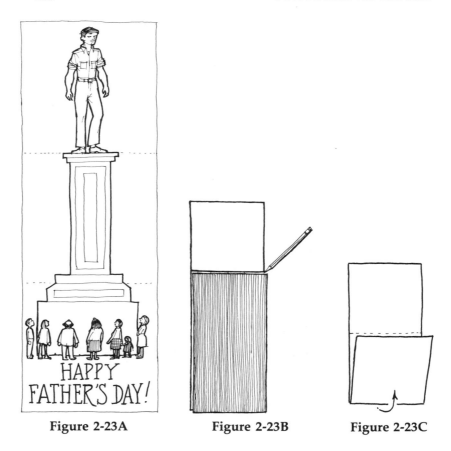

Figure 2-23A   **Figure 2-23B**   **Figure 2-23C**

other side as shown in Figure 2-23C to divide the paper into three equal parts.

2. On the top part of this folded paper have your kids use their black crayons to make a drawing of the "big man" in their lives. *This drawing should be done without background and positioned so that the feet touch the fold.* (See Figure 2-23D.)

3. Now have your kids open this folded paper so that the other two-thirds are visible. On the remaining paper can now be drawn a large and elaborate pedestal to support the completed "statue" of this famous person. (See Figure 2-23A.)

4. When this pedestal is complete, surround the whole area with a sea of admiring people!

Figure 2-23D

TO MAKE THE ENVELOPE

Fold the 6″ × 12″ colored paper in half widthwise and wrap with paper "ribbon" held in place with a dab or two of paste. Use the 2″ × 4″ white paper as a name tag, and add a bow of colored "ribbon" paper.

The results? Judge for yourself! (See Figure 2-23E.)

Figure 2-23E

The word "again" echoed into a repeat
pattern; see Lesson 9, p. 176.

REPEAT THAT AGAIN?

3

The throbbing rhythms of a jungle drum, the interlocking colors of a Black Watch plaid, the sight and sound of cresting and crashing surf: *Repetition* has the power to evoke strong emotions and to give endless pleasure to the senses.

Repetition plays many roles in art, but none so easy to understand, or so accessible to kids, as that of the *repeat pattern*. From the alternating squares of the red and black checkerboard to the mind-boggling flip-flops of the hexaflexagons, this section contains a treasury of child-centered, repeat-pattern lesson plans that will artfully entertain, enrich, and challenge the creative ingenuity of your children.

"Repeat that again?"

STANDARD FARE

Lesson 1   Easy Repeats

Since an activity cannot be fun and boring at the same time, the secret to a nonfail lesson is to eliminate the boring parts, introduce an element of surprise, and make the outcome as attractive as humanly possible. *Easy Repeats* succeeds in all three departments!

YOU NEED:

> assorted construction papers (including black and white)
> 2" × 16"
> 1½" × 12"
> 6" × 8"
> 9" × 12" mounting papers (optional)
>
> scissors
>
> paste or glue

TO PRESENT:

1. Have your kids fold their 2" × 16" papers in half widthwise, unfold, and then fold the sides into the middle as shown in Figures 3-1B and 3-1C.

2. Fold once again from both ends as in Figure 3-1D.

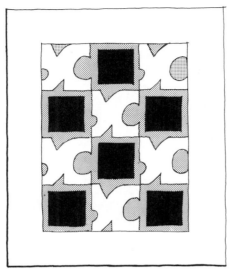

Figure 3-1A

Figure 3-1B

Figure 3-1C

Figure 3-1D

Figure 3-1E

3.   Unfold all folds and cut off the last two squares. Scribble-Cancel* the reverse side of this six-part strip.

4.   Now have your kids refold the six-part strip so that they can cut out a "bite" from each of the four sides as suggested in Figure 3-1E. (Some kids find it easier to first cut through half of this packet and then use the cut-out first half of this packet as a guide for the remaining half.)

5.   Now all that is left to do with this part of the lesson is to unfold, snip off the individual designs, and paste them—corners touching—onto the 6″ × 8″ paper as shown in Figure 3-1F.

6.   Repeat Steps 1, 2, and 3 (without the Scribble-Canceling) with the 1½″ × 12″ paper and then have your kids

---

*See Glossary.

Figure 3-1F

snip off the squares and paste them as shown in Figure 3-1A.

And—if you want to go first class—paste or glue the final product on a 9″ × 12″ mount!

Lesson 2   REPEATING THE SEASONS:
a lesson for Christmas, Valentine's Day, or other seasonal events that can be easily represented by simple cut-out silhouettes*

While unrelieved repetition as shown here in Figure 3-2A is often pleasant enough to *look* at, most kids find this kind of *work* both tedious and boring. With kids, the fun of

Figure 3-2A

*See Suggestions in Figure 3-2C.

working with pattern doesn't even begin until repetition is complemented by contrast. The *Easy Repeats* of the last lesson showed you one way of achieving contrast—here's another!

YOU NEED:

8″ × 12″ drawing paper

six 2″ squares of white paper and twelve of an appropriate seasonal color

2″ × 8″ pattern-weight paperboard

pencils and crayons

paste or glue

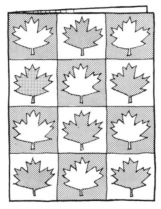

Figure 3-2B

TO PRESENT:

1. Have your kids fold their 8″ × 12″ drawing paper in half widthwise to make the basic card. The 2″ × 8″ paperboards are to be used as Measuring Strips* to subdivide the cover into twelve 2″ squares. Six of the colored paper squares are then pasted or glued in alternating squares, checkerboard-style. (See Figure 3-2D.)

2. Then, using more of the colored paper, have your kids cut out and paste down a holiday motif on each of the white

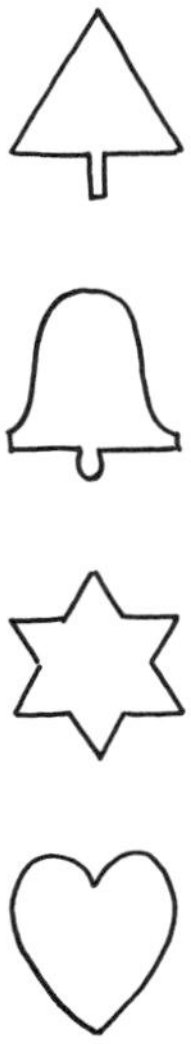

---

*See Glossary.

Figure 3-2C

Figure 3-2D

squares. Cut the same motif from the squares of white paper, and paste these onto the colored squares. (See Figure 3-2A.)

3. Then—invite your kids to open up the inside of the card and to decorate it accordingly!

Envelope Making

Since envelopes are not at all hard to make, this would be as good a time as any to show your kids a very simple but highly effective way of making envelopes.

YOU NEED:

12" × 18" paper
paste or glue
scissors
ruler or Straight-Edge
pencil

TO PRESENT:

1. Position the card to be mailed near the center of the large envelope paper. (See Figure 3-2F.)

---

*See Glossary.

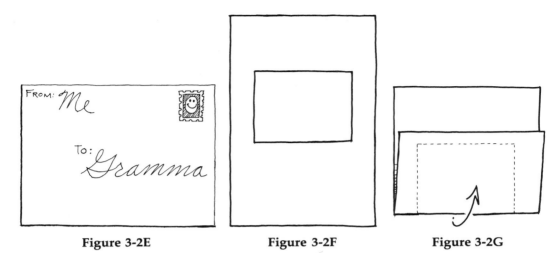

|Figure 3-2E|Figure 3-2F|Figure 3-2G|

2. Fold up the bottom of the envelope paper so that the card is completely hidden (with room to spare). See Figure 3-2G.

3. Fold in the sides of the envelope paper to *loosely* contain the card. (See Figure 3-2H.)

4. Unfold the side folds and fold down the top of the envelope paper as shown in Figure 3-2I.

5. Unfold all folds, draw point of flap with ruler, and Scribble-Cancel* the areas indicated in Figure 3-2J. Cut away scribbled areas.

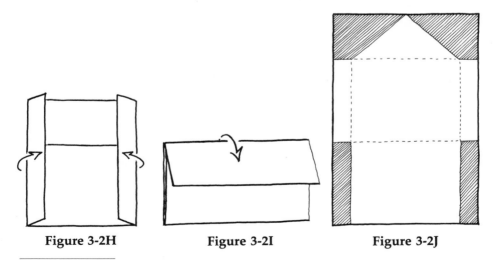

|Figure 3-2H|Figure 3-2I|Figure 3-2J|

*See Glossary.

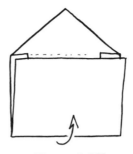

Figure 3-2K

6. Fold in the side flaps and add paste or glue to the top surface of these flaps. Fold up bottom flap and press. (Figure 3-2K.) Envelope is now ready to go. Just have your kids add card, seal, send it to someone they love!

Lesson 3   Back-Rubbed Repeats

In pattern making it is often the very same repetition that pleases the eye that also tires the hand! The secret to the success of these *Back-Rubbed Repeats* lies in the happy knowledge that with every medium comes an insider's trick. The trick to use here is something called *Back-Rubbing*. For a definition of this term, please see the Glossary definition on page 208.

And *then*, hurry back!

FIRST ACTIVITY: INTRODUCTORY BACK-RUB

YOU NEED:

9" × 12" drawing paper

2¼" × 3" tagboard (or any other sturdy, lightweight paperboard)

crayons

Back-Rubbers

Figure 3-3A

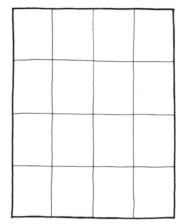

Figure 3-3B

TO PRESENT:

1. Have your kids fold their 9″ × 12″ papers into 16ths* as shown here in Figure 3-3B.

2. A simple line drawing is then heavily crayoned onto the 2¼″ × 3″ paperboard.

3. Once these line drawings are completed, invite your kids to Back-Rub their crayoned designs, checkerboard style, onto their prepared drawing paper. While the Back-Rubbed pattern itself may or may not have to be touched up with additional crayon, the imperfect transferred designs will definitely need a certain amount of touching up. These designs can then be either left as is or decorated with crayon.

4. The remaining areas are then crayoned in to complete this simple alternate repeat. (See Figure 3-3A.)

5. Display and admire!

---

*See Glossary for *Paper Folding*.

SECOND ACTIVITY: THE FULL-LENGTH BACK-RUB

YOU NEED:

12″ × 16″ drawing paper
pattern-weight paperboard: 8″ × 16″ and 4″ squares
crayons
Back-Rubber

Figure 3-3C

TO PRESENT:

1. Have your kids use their 8″ × 16″ paperboard as a Measuring Strip* to divide their 12″ × 16″ paper into lightly penciled thirds as indicated in Figure 3-3D.

2. Discuss with your kids the meaning of the word *theme*. Once they understand this concept, have them use their 4″ squares of paperboard to design two different design ideas that echo the same theme.

---

*See Glossary.

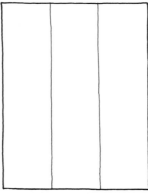

Figure 3-3D

3. The rest is easy: Using their patterns as the basis for an alternate repeat design, they can Back-Rub these designs into alternate squares as suggested in Figure 3-3C. Touch up as needed and admire!

Lesson 4 The Borderline

Like everything else, patterns are subject to the whims of style and taste. By the time a style is so old that it is only dimly remembered—presto!—it's back again, rediscovered by the tastemakers, forgiven of its past sins and excesses, and once again venerated as a respectable and fashionable art form!

When I was a kid, *borders* were an integral part of a designer's bag of tricks. Borders were used to decorate everything from public buildings to books. Back then, even our living quarters sported border designs along our papered walls to accentuate the separation of the patterned wallpaper from the painted ceiling.

A border revival is long overdue, and since it has to start somewhere, how would you and your kids like to be remembered as the characters who led the parade?

"Who are those kids?"

"Hey—they're the bunch that made it *all* happen!"

FIRST ACTIVITY: SERPENTINE DESIGNS

YOU NEED:

> 3″ × 18″ and 4″ × 18″ construction paper in assorted colors
>
> 3″ × 18″ white drawing paper
>
> scissors
>
> paste or glue

Figure 3-4A

TO PRESENT:

1. Have your kids fold their 3″ × 18″ colored paper in half widthwise, and once again as shown in Figures 3-4B and 3-4C.

2. Being careful not to cut any of the folded edges completely away, cut the folded paper "snowflake style" as suggested here in Figure 3-4D.

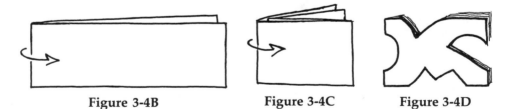

Figure 3-4B   **Figure 3-4C**   **Figure 3-4D**

3. Open up the cut paper design and paste or glue to the 3″ × 18″ white paper. Paste this subassembly to the larger colored paper as shown in Figure 3-4A. That's it!

SECOND ACTIVITY: HORIZON DESIGNS

YOU NEED:

3″ × 6″ lightweight paperboard
3″ × 18″ drawing paper
4″ × 18″ construction paper for mounting
crayons
Back-Rubbers*

Figure 3-4E

TO PRESENT:

1. Explain to your kids the concept of a *horizon line*. Explain that in this activity the horizon line can be as flat as still water or as angular as the Rocky Mountains, but whatever their decision, this horizon line must start and stop at points equally distant from the bottom of the 3″ × 6″ paperboard pattern. (An easy way to assure accuracy is to have your kids use a piece of scrap paper as a measuring and transferring device. (See Figure 3-4F.)

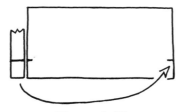

Figure 3-4F

---

*See Glossary, *Back-Rubbing*.

2. The only restrictions that must be observed here are that no part of the picture must touch the ends of the pattern except the horizon line, and that this drawing is best done in heavily applied crayon line. Shown here are two sample ideas. (See Figures 3-4G and 3-4H.)

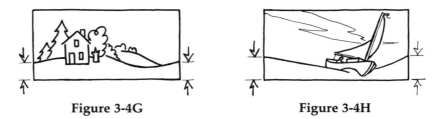

Figure 3-4G   Figure 3-4H

3. The rest is easy: Simply follow the instructions found on page 208 for Back-Rubbing these designs onto the 3″ × 18″ drawing paper, touch up with crayon and enjoy!

FREAKING OUT

In my first Parker book, *Paste, Pencils, Scissors and Crayons*, I outlined the bare bones of a lesson I called *Freak-Outs*. Since this introductory lesson did little more than hint at the full potential of the Freak-Out principle, I have decided to take this space to proudly introduce you to the full flowering of this beguiling art form.

Lesson 5   Line-Outs

Most Freak-Out lessons can be enjoyed by kids of almost any age, but—with *little* kids—Line-Outs work best of all!

YOU NEED:

6″ squares of drawing paper
crayons
Back-Rubbers*

---

*See Glossary for *Back-Rubbing*.

Figure 3-5A

TO PRESENT:

ACTIVITY NUMBER ONE: BASIC LINE-OUTS

1. Have your kids fold their papers in half. Their first assignment: to use their crayons to draw a heavy random line that starts on the fold and ends on the fold. (See Figure 3-5B.)

Figure 3-5B

2. The Freak-Out is then turned inside out and Back-Rubbed as shown in Figure 3-5C.

3. When your kids unfold their Freak-Outs, they will be delighted to discover that their random lines have been magically transformed into closed figures. Invite your kids to darken the imperfect side of this transference and—with that—their introduction to the Freak-Out will have been successfully negotiated! (See Figure 3-5A.)

Figure 3-5C

ACTIVITY NUMBER TWO: COLORED LINE-OUTS

1. Have your kids fold another one of their 6" squares in half, and again draw a heavy random line that starts on the fold and ends on the fold. However—this time invite them to add another random line in another color (as suggested in Figure 3-5D). Reverse the fold, Back-Rub, open up and look again! This time your children will be delighted to find *two* overlapping figures!

Figure 3-5D

2. Invite your kids to again darken the imperfect side

Figure 3-5E

and—if so inclined—to color in these Colored Line-Outs. (See Figure 3-5E.)

ACTIVITY NUMBER THREE: BORDER LINE-OUTS

YOU NEED:

2″ × 18″ drawing paper

crayons

Back-Rubbers

Figure 3-5F

TO PRESENT:

1. Have your kids fold their papers in half widthwise, then open them up and fold the ends into the middle. Unfold.

2. Instruct your kids to draw one or more "interesting" lines from side to side in either one of the two end sections as suggested in Figure 3-5G.

3. Once the decorative lines have been drawn, fold the end section over its neighboring section, and transfer the

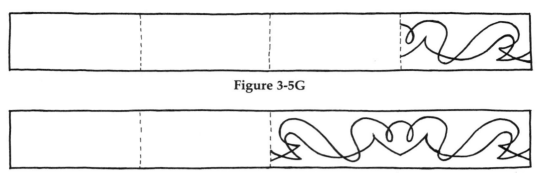

Figure 3-5G

Figure 3-5H

image by Back-Rubbing. Open up and touch up with crayon. (See Figure 3-5H.)

4. Now that one half of the design is complete, fold over the crayoned half and Back-Rub the image onto the remaining half. Open up, touch up with crayon, and admire! (See Figure 3-5F.)

ACTIVITY NUMBER FOUR: BORDER LINE-OUTS SUPREME

Once your kids are familiar with what to expect from the Border Line-Outs, it is time to reintroduce the idea of a pictorial border.

The basic design units shown here (see Figures 3-5I and 3-5J) and the accompanying border designs (Figures 3-5K

Figure 3-5I

Figure 3-5J

and 3-5L) are adapted from the illustrations on page 160, but here—by reversing the image—a whole *new* scene develops!

Figure 3-5K

Figure 3-5L

ACTIVITY NUMBER FIVE: ADVANCED LINE-OUTS

By this time it is a pretty dull kid who hasn't gotten the idea. *Now* is the time for you to begin to make your exit from center stage. They have seen enough of you—what they need is a chance to experiment on their own. Pass out more paper of all shapes and sizes and let your kids begin to experiment on their own.

Your job here is done!

Lesson 6   **Easy-Outs**

Whereas *little* kids are quite satisfied with the *Line-Outs* of the previous lesson, the *Easy-Outs* are—by far—the all-time favorite for everybody else!

YOU NEED:

drawing paper in the following sizes:
4½″ × 12″
6″ squares
9″ squares
8½″ circle patterns
crayons, scissors, and Back-Rubbers

TO PRESENT:

FIRST ACTIVITY: HALF-FREAKS

1. Just as in the *Basic Line-Out* lesson (page 161), have your kids fold one of the 6″ square papers in half, and draw in some sort of a design that touches the fold. (See Figure 3-6A.) However, this time suggest to your kids that they limit their colors to two, or, at the most, three. Again—a heavy hand here will pay off in a higher quality transferred image.

2. Turn the paper inside out, Back-Rub, open up, touch up with crayons and applaud! (See Figure 3-6B.)

Figure 3-6A

Figure 3-6B

ACTIVITY NUMBER TWO: QUADRANT FREAKS

1. Have your kids take another 6″ square of paper but this time fold the paper into quarters. Instruct them to use their crayons to decorate one quadrant in such a way so that some parts of this decoration are touching the folded lines as suggested in Figure 3-6C.

Figure 3-6C

2. When this quadrant design is complete, have your kids fold the paper in half and Back-Rub. When the resulting transfer has been touched up, fold the total crayoned half against the total uncrayoned half and Back-Rub again. The final results are always a great success! (See Figure 3-6D.)

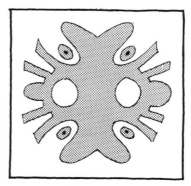

Figure 3-6D

ACTIVITY NUMBER THREE: TRIANGLE FREAKS

Figure 3-6E

Many concepts that we take so much for granted are still brand new to those learning them for the first time. One demonstration of this can be seen when you ask a child to repeat the same basic instructions given above for the *Quadrant Freaks* for a 6" square of paper folded into *diagonal* quarters! (See Figures 3-6E and 3-6F.)

Figure 3-6F

ACTIVITY NUMBER FOUR: RECTANGLE FREAKS

Once *you* understand the concept, my instructions can become shorter and shorter!

For *Rectangle Freaks* fold the 9″ × 4½″ paper into four linear quarters and proceed as in the previous activities to arrive at an attractive linear design. (See Figure 3-6G.)

Figure 3-6G

ACTIVITY NUMBER FIVE: CIRCLE FREAKS

Since this activity is often more successful when approached as line design, by definition it should more properly be included among the *Line-Outs* on pp. 160-164. However—the concepts involved here are just a little too complex for very little children and are therefore better saved for the more experienced *Freak-Out* player.

Figure 3-6H

1. Have your kids trace the circle patterns onto their 9″ squares. Cut out these circles, fold them into eight parts and decorate them with crayons as suggested in Figure 3-6I. Naturally some parts of the decoration must touch the folded lines.

Figure 3-6I

2. Then proceed in Freak-Out fashion until the design has traveled around the circle! (See Figure 3-6H.)

3. Since this concept is a little more difficult for kids to understand than the others in this lesson, you might find it necessary to Quarterback* this one!

Lesson 7   **Way-Outs**

Now that you have tried out the ideas presented in Lessons 5 and 6, you and your kids should be more than ready to begin to experiment with some of your more ambitious Freak-Out ideas. Here are some of my favorites!

YOU NEED:

drawing paper in the following sizes:
9″ squares
4½″ × 12″
crayons
Back-Rubbers**

---

*See Glossary.

**See Glossary for *Back-Rubbing*.

TO PRESENT:

FIRST ACTIVITY: BENT FREAKS

1. Have your kids fold one of their 9" squares into four quadrants. Unfold. Fold one of the corners into the middle. Unfold. Invite your kids to decorate the bent corner in such a way so that part of the design touches not only the fold but the two outside edges as well. (See Figure 3-7B.)

Figure 3-7A

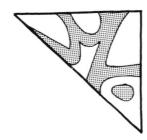

Figure 3-7B

2. Using the concept mastered in the last two lessons, the corner design is transferred to the adjoining triangle and from there transferred to the rest of the paper. (See procedure under *Quadrant Freaks,* p. 165.)

3. The results are usually quite spectacular! (See Figure 3-7A.)

SECOND ACTIVITY: PIECES OF EIGHT

Another good one is this: have your kids fold their 4½" × 12" papers into eighths and invite your kids to decorate one of the corner rectangles in such a way that the crayoned design touches both folds and the short edge. (See Figure 3-7D.) Then transfer this design to its vertical neighbor as shown in Figure 3-7E. From there on follow the instructions outlined in Rectangle Freaks, p. 167. (See Figure 3-7C.)

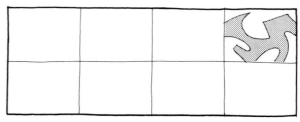

Figure 3-7C

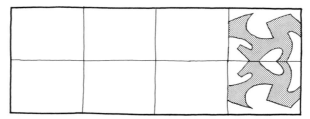

Figure 3-7D

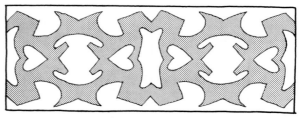

Figure 3-7E

THIRD ACTIVITY: DOUBLE-CROSSERS

1. Using another 9″ square, have your kids fold it horizontally, vertically, and diagonally as shown in Figure 3-7F.*

2. Then decorate one of these triangular shapes in such a way that part of the design touches each of the folded edges. (See Figure 3-7G.)

3. This Freak-Out is then completed in a manner identical to that given in the directions for the *Circle Freaks* on page 167. (See Figure 3-7A.)

---

*See Glossary for *Paper Folding*.

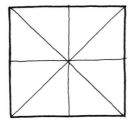

Figure 3-7F

Figure 3-7G

NAME CALLING

We may like our names or we may hate our names but names are never just *words*. And what is true of names in general is particularly true of our first names. Not only are these emotionally charged symbols seen as considerably larger than life, but they are often viewed with a fascination that borders on the mystical. Take these names and begin to turn them into repeat patterns, and slowly, right before your eyes—will emerge a fabric of pure magic.

Lesson 8   **Tie Downs**

A great favorite of the cottage industry craftspeople is the handpainted tie that uses one's name as the basis for a highly decorative and unusual design motif. While *few* of your kids may want to go so far as to chance the kind of misadventures that can take place when one bends over an expensive tie with a dripping brush in hand, *all* will delight in learning how to make these *Tie Downs* on paper.

ACTIVITY NUMBER ONE: FIRST DOWNS

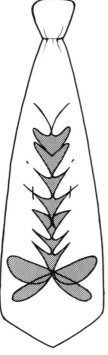

Figure 3-8A

YOU NEED:

4½" × 12" drawing paper

crayons

Back-Rubber*

PREPARATION:

I find that this kind of a lesson gets off to a better start if I preface it by making a sample Tie Down to show the kids. Here's how I do it:

1. I fold the paper lengthwise and unfold. Then I choose a name (my name, your name, anybody's name) and write this name in crayon in such a way that the bottom of each letter touches the folded line. (See Figure 3-8B.)

2. I then refold the paper so that the name is sandwiched between the two halves and use a Back-Rubber to transfer the crayoned image to the other side of the folded paper. When I open up and complete this transfer with the help of a little crayon touchup, the resulting image will look something like that shown in Figure 3-8C.

3. To finish this design I then color it in as shown in Figure 3-8A. (Cutting it out in the shape of a tie is, of course, optional!)

TO PRESENT:

1. Call the attention of your class to your prepared Tie Down and ask them what it "says." With one or more

*See Glossary under *Back-Rubbing*.

Figure 3-8B **Figure 3-8C**

prepared Tie Downs a great deal of good-natured classroom fun can be engaged in if this part of the lesson is turned into a guessing game in which those who learn to decipher the "code" are instructed to keep the secret to themselves until all the children have had a chance to figure it out for themselves!

2. Once the secret is understood by all, simply pass out the necessary materials and turn your class loose to make their own Tie Downs!

ACTIVITY NUMBER TWO: SECOND DOWNS

Once the basic *Tie Down* of the previous activity is understood, there is no limit to the kinds of variations that are possible!

YOU NEED:

6″ × 18″ drawing paper
crayons and Back-Rubber

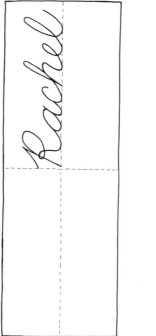

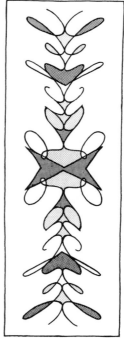

| **Figure 3-8D** | **Figure 3-8E** |

TO PRESENT:

1. Have your kids fold their papers into quarters and write their names in crayon in such a way that the first letter touches the short central fold, and so that the bottom of each letter touches the long central fold. (See Figure 3-8D.)

2. Then in the manner in which designs were transferred in the *Quadrant Freaks* on page 165, Back-Rub the design until it looks something like that pictured in Figure 3-8E.

3. Color and confound!

ACTIVITY NUMBER THREE: THIRD DOWNS

And finally, here is as complicated a *Tie Down* as anyone could wish for!

Figure 3-8F

YOU NEED:

12″ square of drawing paper

scissors

crayons

Back-Rubber

TO PRESENT:

1. Invite your kids to fold their 12″ square drawing papers into eight parts exactly the same way as explained in the Double-Crossers on page 170.

2. Once the paper is folded as shown, have your kids place their names touching both sides of the "piece of pie" as suggested in Figure 3-8G.

3. Then—Freak-Out style (see earlier lessons)—transfer this initial design around the central pivot. Decorate and contemplate! (See Figure 3-8F.)

Figure 3-8G

Lesson 9   Echoes

Of all the *Name Calling* lessons, I guess I have to admit that this one is *my* favorite!

YOU NEED:

9″ × 12″ or 6″ × 18″ drawing paper
pencils and crayons
Back-Rubbers*

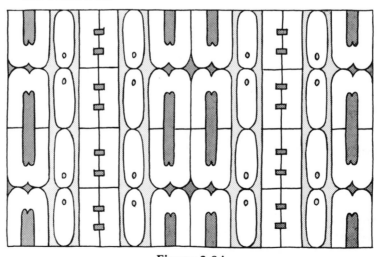

Figure 3-9A

---

*See Glossary.

TO PRESENT:

1. Give those children with long first names the 6″ × 18″ drawing paper; those with short first names, the 9″ × 12″ paper.

2. Carefully folding one fold at a time, your kids then fold their papers in sixteen parts as shown in Figure 3-9B. (Also see Paper Folding in the Glossary.)

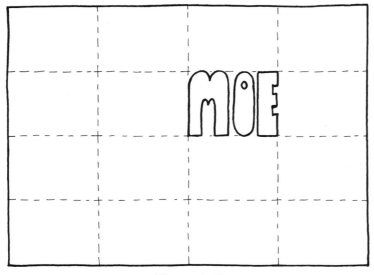

Figure 3-9B

3. Using "fat" letters, your kids can jam the name into one of the sixteen parts. Have them do this in pencil and have them do it in such a way that the name touches *all* sides of the rectangular enclosure.

4. Once these instructions have been carried out, have your kids darken the outlines of the letters.

5. Then—using the standard Freak-Out procedures explained earlier in this chapter—have your kids transfer this name design to all the remaining boxes on their paper.

When done, encourage them to color or decorate these designs in any way they choose. *Everybody* will be delighted with the results! (See Figure 3-9A and the lead illustration to this section.)

"CUT THAT OUT!"*

Easy to use, yet incredibly decorative, cut paper is the perfect medium for repeat designs!

Lesson 10   Simple Cut-Ups

To take space here to discuss some of the best of the cut paper, repeat-pattern lessons for the lower-primary grades would be to face the accusation that I am repeating material I included in *Paste, Pencils, Scissors and Crayons*.** On the other hand, not giving *some* mention of these great primary classics is inviting the counteraccusation that I have neglected to inform the readers of some of the great lessons that might be missing. Since I am damned if I do and damned if I don't—I'll take affirmative action and *do it*!

YOU NEED:

> strips and squares of lightweight paper (duplicating and mimeograph paper works well here!)
>
> scissors
>
> pencil

ACTIVITY NUMBER ONE: SNOW TIME

The basic "snowflake" is nothing more than a square folded into quarters with pieces cut out of it. (See Figures 3-10A and 3-10B.) With little kids you will have fewer failures if you instruct them to cut only one "bite" out of each side.

---

*After the initial instructions in a cut paper lesson have been explained to kids of lower-elementary school age, the mock-tyrannical command of "CUT THAT OUT!" will at first stun, and then provoke spontaneous laughter as, one by one, the kids catch on that "cut that out!" is nothing more than an invitation to use their scissors.

You don't think this is funny? *I* don't think this is funny. But kids? *They* think it's hysterical!

**Parker Publishing Co., Inc., 1979.

Figure 3-10A   **Figure 3-10B**

When finished, display as is or mount on dark, colored paper.

A novel variation that can be done with this design is to cut the finished product apart on the folded lines and mount on a slightly larger sheet of dark construction paper as shown in Figure 3-10C. (Prefolding the mounting paper in quarters makes the positioning easier.)

With older kids the "snowflake" can be folded one more time and the cuts can be more adventurous. (See Figures 3-10D and 3-10E.) Mounted on dark, colored paper, these designs always make an attractive display.

Figure 3-10C   **Figure 3-10D**

Figure 3-10E

ACTIVITY NUMBER TWO: STRIP MINING

While this section has already given recognition to the merits of cut paper border repeats (see p. 164), these repeats need not be abstract. (See lead illustration for this section.)

The easiest kind of Strip Mining Repeats uses the double-fold unit shown in Figures 3-10G and 3-10H (only). The more complicated ones use the three-fold unit shown in Figure 3-10I. Either way, these border repeats are always fun to do. (See Figure 3-10F.)*

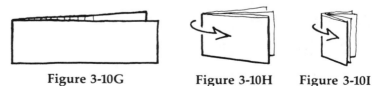

Figure 3-10F

Figure 3-10G   **Figure 3-10H**   **Figure 3-10I**

*Also see suggestions on page 97 of my *Paste, Pencils, Scissors & Crayons*.

Lesson 11   Figure and Ground Repeats

Figure and ground are words dear to the hearts of psychologists and others concerned with matters of perception. In the silhouette here at the right, the figure is the "bottle," the ground the "space" around it.

Figure 3-11A

However, once the representational elements are removed and the figure and ground given equal or near-equal weight, the whole idea of one shape being the figure and the other the ground becomes more a matter of recreational perception than a matter of psychological concern! (See Figures 3-11B through 3-11F.)

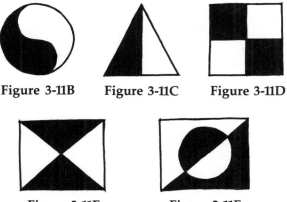

Figure 3-11B   **Figure 3-11C**   **Figure 3-11D**

Figure 3-11E   **Figure 3-11F**

ACTIVITY NUMBER ONE: GROUND BREAKING

YOU NEED:

12" × 18" construction paper in assorted colors.

TO PRESENT:

1. Invite your kids to choose two sheets of colored construction paper. Since pieces of one sheet will eventually be pasted on top of the other, explain that the two sheets should have enough contrast to look good.

2. Have your kids fold one of the sheets in half lengthwise and then cut large pieces out of this fold in such a way that no two pieces touch one another. (See Figure 3-11H.) Open up and cut on the center fold. *Save all parts.*

Figure 3-11G   **Figure 3-11H**

3. Now comes the first real problem. You and I can see what needs to be done by looking at Figure 3-11G, but even if you covered the walls of your room with these *Ground Breaking* designs, your kids are still going to need all the help they can get. Here is the best way that I have found to do it:

Ask your kids to choose one of the two larger pieces and to paste this piece down as shown in Figure 3-11I. Once this

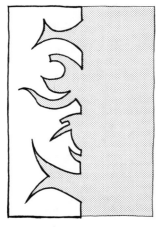

Figure 3-11I

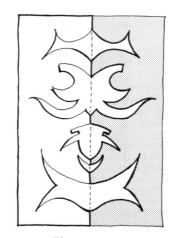

Figure 3-11J

piece is in place, have them place (not paste) the cut-out pieces in position as shown in Figure 3-11J. Then—paste down that part of each cut-out that extends beyond the center fold. Cut away the other half. (See Figure 3-11G.)

4. And that's it. Display and admire!

ACTIVITY NUMBER TWO: PLAY GROUNDS

Once you and your kids understand the basic concepts involved, there is no end to the complexity of the designs that one can make. The temptation, however, is to attempt too much too soon. While *Play Grounds* may not seem to be that much more difficult to do than the previous activity, I can state from ample experience that—for kids—some of these *Figure and Ground Repeats* are not as easy as they look!

YOU NEED:

the same needs list as was used in the first activity

TO PRESENT:

1. Begin as in the previous activity but this time instruct your kids to continue cutting out designs around the total perimeter of the folded paper. (See Figure 3-11L.)

Figure 3-11K   **Figure 3-11L**

2. Continue as in Step 3 of the previous activity by pasting down one of the large pieces and pasting in the opposite center parts.

3. For the final paste and assembling job, have your kids lay down the other half piece (*without* paste!) and use this piece as a guide for pasting in the final pieces to complete the design. (See Figures 3-11M and 3-11K.)

Figure 3-11M

ACTIVITY NUMBER THREE: FORE-GROUNDS

While *Figure and Ground Designs* can become as ambitious as the kids with whom you are working, the quadrant-fold design given below is as complicated as anything you and your kids will probably ever care to try. It's hard—but it's beautiful!

YOU NEED:

12″ squares of construction paper in assorted colors
scissors and paste or glue

Figure 3-11N

TO PRESENT:

1. Have your kids fold one of the 12″ squares of construction paper into quarters. This folded packet is then cut on all four sides as suggested in Figure 3-11O. Again—*save all parts*.

2. Open up and carefully label each quadrant with an identifying number before cutting apart. (Otherwise it is very easy to become hopelessly confused!)

Figure 3-11O

3. Then, using the experience gained from working with easier *Figure and Ground Repeats*, assemble and paste! (See Figure 3-11N.)

CARD REPEATS

One of the secrets of conducting successful repeat-pattern lessons is to use nothing but easy-to-make, easy-to-use patterns. Earlier in this section I introduced you to *Back-Rubbed* patterns and cut-paper patterns, here's one more trick to add to your repertoire: I call these things *Card Repeats*— and you'll soon see why!

Lesson 12   Simple Card Repeats

In its simplest form the *Card Repeat* is nothing more than a pattern cut from tagboard, bristol board, or any other sturdy, lightweight paperboard that can be used for pattern making or stenciling.

Here are two of the best *Card Repeats:*

ACTIVITY NUMBER ONE: PLAYING YOUR CARDS

YOU NEED:

patternweight paperboard:
   3″ squares (two each)
   3″ × 15″
   6″ × 15″

assorted colors of construction paper:

   3″ squares

   12″ × 15″

scissors and pencils

paste or glue

Figure 3-12A

TO PRESENT:

1. Have your kids use their 3″ × 15″ and their 6″ × 15″ Measuring Strips* to lightly subdivide their 12″ × 15″ colored construction paper into 3″ squares.

2. The 3″ paperboard squares are then cut into any kind of a freely designed shape. This shape must observe only one rule: one part of each edge must be kept intact. (See Figures 3-12B, 3-12C, and 3-12D for suggestions.)

3. These paperboard patterns are then repeatedly traced on 3″ squares of colored construction paper, and the construction paper designs are then cut out and assembled into repeat patterns on the 12″ × 15″ paper and pasted in place as in Figure 3-12A.

Then mount on larger pieces of paper and display!

These patterns can be as varied in design and color as the imagination allows. Here, in Figures 3-12E and 3-12F are examples of some of the possible variations.

Figure 3-12B

Figure 3-12C

Figure 3-12D

---

*See Glossary.

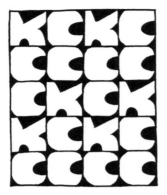

Figure 3-12E

Figure 3-12F

ACTIVITY NUMBER TWO: STENCILED REPEATS

YOU NEED:

pattern-weight paperboard Measuring Strips:
$1\frac{1}{2}'' \times 6''$, $3'' \times 15''$, $9'' \times 15''$, and 6″ squares
12″ × 15″ light-colored drawing or construction paper
Paper-Poker
pencils, scissors, and crayons

Figure 3-12G

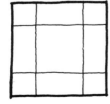

Figure 3-12H

TO PRESENT:

1. Have your kids use their $1\frac{1}{2}'' \times 6''$ Measuring Strips on one (or more) of the 6″ squares to rule out the grid shown here in Figure 3-12H.

2. Your kids are then invited to use the center section of this grid to draw in some kind of a complicated design that will be easy to cut out. (See Figures 3-12I, 3-12J, and 3-12K for suggestions.)

When they are done, they can use some kind of a Paper-Poker* to puncture a hole in the center of their design to enable their scissors to make entry. Cut away the interior of the design and save the grid.

3. With the help of the 9" × 15" and the 3" × 15" Measuring Strips, your kids can divide their drawing paper into 3" squares (Figure 3-12L). Then, using the penciled lines on the paperboard stencil pattern as positioning aids, stencil in the desired pattern as suggested in Figure 3-12M.

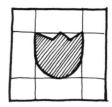

Figure 3-12I

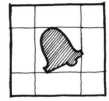

Figure 3-12J

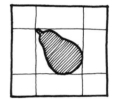

Figure 3-12K

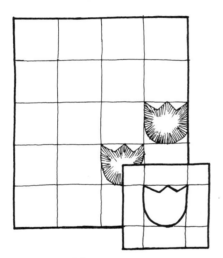

Figure 3-12L

Figure 3-12M

INTERLOCKING REPEATS

The construction of *Interlocking Repeats,* or *plane tessela-tions* (as the mathematicians refer to them) has to be one of the design world's best-kept secrets. While known for centuries by the Moorish artists who turned their creative talents to mosaic tile, and more recently by M. C. Escher, the 20th century Dutch artist who lifted the periodic division of the

*See Glossary.

plane from the realm of the purely decorative and transformed it into his own private world of fantasy, very few commoners (like ourselves) have ever been initiated into the secrets that command this most fascinating of diversions. But now the secret's out and it's *our* job to share the good news!

The principle may well belong to the ages—but *this* presentation is *brand new*!

Lesson 13   The Two-Way Interlocking Repeat

Many repeat patterns are easy to do, or at least easy to figure out—but for most people the crazy, altered squares that are the subject of this lesson need not only an explanation but a *modus operandi*—you have to know *how* to do them, and this is where *this* lesson saves the day!

YOU NEED:

pattern-weight paperboard in the following sizes:
  3″ square
  3″ × 4½″
  3″ × 6″
construction paper in the following colors and sizes:
  3″ × 18″ white or colored
  6″ × 9″ in a contrasting color
  4″ × 18″ dark-colored mounting paper
pencils, scissors, and paste or glue

Figure 3-13A

TO PRESENT:

1. The 3" square is placed at the bottom of the 3" × 4½" pattern board and traced as shown here in Figure 3-13B. A free-flowing line is then drawn connecting the two top corners of the traced square as suggested here in Figure 3-13C.* Cut out on this new line.

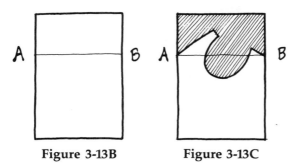

Figure 3-13B   **Figure 3-13C**

2. This "half-pattern" is then cut out and placed at the top of the 3" × 6" patternboard and traced as shown here in Figure 3-13D. Now comes the only tricky part of the whole operation. Have your kids slide down their "half-pattern" so that the straight line A-B coincides with straight line C-D. When this alignment is complete, the cut-out line is traced in this position. See Figure 3-13E. Then—cut out the whole pattern as indicated in Figure 3-13F.

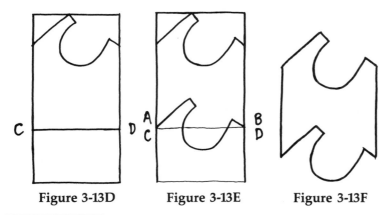

Figure 3-13D   **Figure 3-13E**   **Figure 3-13F**

*Since this free-flowing line is to be cut out and used as a pattern, discourage your kids from drawing a line that is unnecessarily complicated!

3. This completed pattern is cut out and traced about four times on the 6″ × 9″ colored construction paper and the resulting tracings also cut out. The rest is easy: Using the master pattern as a spacer, the colored paper cut-outs are then pasted to the 3″ × 18″ paper as shown in Figure 3-13G.

Figure 3-13G

And with that—your introduction to the world of the Interlocking Repeat is ready for mounting on the 4″ × 18″ paper as shown in Figure 3-13A!

Lesson 14   Doubling the Fun: The Four-Way Interlocking Repeats

Once you and your kids understand the principles underlying the structure of the *Two-Way Interlocking Repeats*, you're only two short steps away from mastering the famous, *Four-Way Interlocking Repeat*!

YOU NEED:

   pattern-weight paperboard in the following sizes:
   3″ square
   4½″ × 6″
   6″ square
8½″ × 11″ (+ or −) practice paper
12″ × 18″ colored construction paper
9″ × 12″ black construction paper—or preferably—black cardboard
pencils, scissors, paste or glue

Figure 3-14A

PRELIMINARY COMMENTS

While there is nothing about this art activity that is difficult to do, there *are* many small steps that must be done in order. I prefer to Quarterback* this activity: you may like to do the same!

TO PRESENT:

1. Have your kids begin by tracing the three-inch-square pattern in one of the corners of the 4½″ × 6″ paperboard. Then have them draw free-flowing lines from each of the "free" corners as suggested in Figure 3-14B.

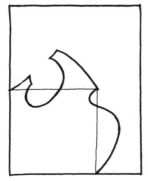

Figure 3-14B

---

*See Glossary for *Quarterbacking*.

2. These "half-patterns" are then cut out and placed in a corner of a 6″ square in such a way that both irregular edges are bordering the outside of the square as shown in Figure 3-14C. Trace.

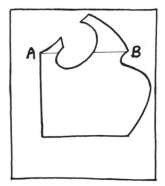

Figure 3-14C

3. Now come the two crucial steps. Straight line A-B is dropped down so that it coincides with straight line C-D so that the cut edge A-B can be traced in this position as shown in Figure 3-14D.

The same procedural steps are now repeated using lines B-D and A-C as shown in Figure 3-14E.

Important Information

While Step 3 above is *seemingly* foolproof, problems do arise in this manner—it sometimes happens that the lines from the two sets overlap as shown in Figure 3-14F.

While this problem is easily remedied, it will also need *your* individual attention. (*This* is one reason why I like to Quarterback this activity!) To solve this kind of problem, simply trim back whatever protuberance is causing the trouble and repair the profiles of the twin outlines so that they are again identical as shown here in Figure 3-14G.

---

4. Once the pattern is completed and cut out, have your kids try it out on practice paper so that they can see for themselves how these repeats interlock in all directions. (See Figure 3-14H.)

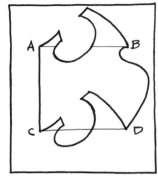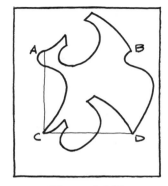

Figure 3-14D   **Figure 3-14E**

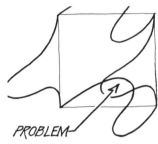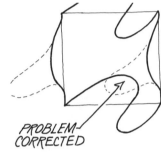

Figure 3-14F   **Figure 3-14G**

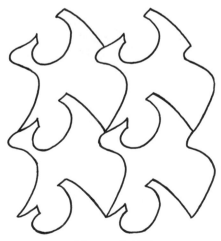

Figure 3-14H

If all is in order, have your kids trace this pattern on the black paper or cardboard to completely fill it with interlocking repeats.

5. The 12" × 18" colored construction paper is then used to make multiple (noninterlocking) tracings of the master pattern. These colored shapes are then cut out and pasted onto the black background as shown in Figure 3-14A.

Lesson 15   Interlocking, Wall-to-Wall People, Creatures, and Things!

Figure 3-15A

One of the great joys of the *Interlocking Repeats* is the ease with which these designs adapt themselves to subject matter, for almost every plane tesselation lends itself to some kind of imaginative treatment. Using nothing more than visual imagination, a great many people have no trouble at all in "seeing" all kinds of outrageous pictures in these simple repeats. In Figures 3-15B – 3-15F can be seen a simple—chosen at random—design followed by some of the many interpretations possible.

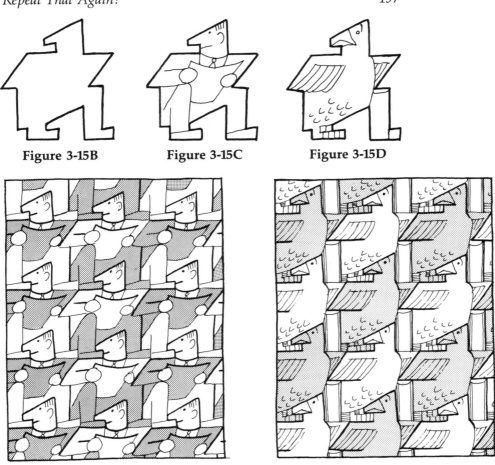

Figure 3-15B   **Figure 3-15C**   **Figure 3-15D**

Figure 3-15E   **Figure 3-15F**

Children who are attracted to this kind of imaginative projection will readily welcome the following suggestions:

Complete your design as in *Doubling the Fun* (Lesson 14). Then, to give these designs representational life, use a black pen to add the details on the colored construction paper and a white pencil to draw the details on the black paper or cardboard. (See Figure 3-15A.)

THE MIND-BLOWING FLEXAGONS!

If someone were to put a gun to my head and a paper and pencil in my hand and snarl, "Give me a list of your all-

Figure 3-16A

time favorite art activities," I'm convinced that my nervous hand would quickly scribble out: *Picnic Lunch,* and any of the *Smile!* "camera" lessons described in *Paste, Pencils, Scissors and Crayons;* the *Two-Timers* and the *Pop-Up* lessons from *Imaginative Art Lessons for Kids and Their Teachers;* and, of course, *The Mind-Blowing Flexagons!* that follow.

The *flexagon* is a decorated, folded-paper hexagon that has some most unusual properties: When manipulated (flexed) in a certain way, this hexagonal paper flower repeatedly opens in ever-changing geometric blooms, sloughing off designs as soon as newer ones appear, a kaleidoscopic surface transformation that continues to entertain and delight long beyond the child's most imaginative expectations.

Invented in 1939 by Arthur H. Stone,* and enjoyed by generations of mathematicians, the hexagon experience is

---

*For an informative and highly entertaining account of the hexagon, see Martin Gardner's *Mathematical Puzzles and Diversions.*

one not easily forgotten. My contribution to flexagon theory is nil, but by organizing and simplifying the flexagon instructions into a highly successful classroom lesson plan, the following pages should do more to introduce this activity to children than all the flexagon articles in all the scientific journals have done to date. And *that* would be no small achievement!

Now for the bad news: Without a great deal of preparation on your part, the making of flexagons probably requires more fine-line accuracy and fine motor skills than most children possess.

Now the good news: With preparation time, a sharp pencil and a yardstick or a long ruler, you can pencil in just enough of the high tolerance work so that the success of this activity is *absolutely* assured!

Lesson 16 The Flexagon—Standard Model

There are all kinds of Flexagons, some much too complicated for classroom use. This one, however, is *my* favorite— you'll soon see why!

PREPARATION:

Standard classroom "art" paper comes in three sizes: 9" × 12", 12" × 18", and 18" × 24". Since the 9" × 12" papers are too small to use for flexagons, I will give you a choice between a medium-size flexagon and a larger one. Relative merits? The medium-size one is easier to prepare; the larger one is showier. Your choice?

THE MEDIUM-SIZE FLEXAGON

Using a sharp pencil and an oversized ruler or yardstick, prepare your 12" × 18" paper with horizontal lines drawn 1½" apart and *very light* vertical lines drawn ⅞" apart. (See Figure 3-16B.)

Now—using this prepared sheet as a master, lay out enough additional sheets to serve the needs of your kids. Count on using at least two strips per child.

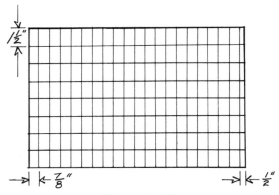

Figure 3-16B

Carefully cut out the long strips, preferably with a paper cutter and distribute them to your class members.

A Word of Caution: Whether you make the medium-size flexagon or the larger flexagon, be sure to save your master, for if you don't use it again today—you'll be using it again soon in the near future!

THE LARGER FLEXAGON

Because quality (nonbowed) yardsticks or meter sticks are not always available when you need them, the larger flexagon is that much harder to make.* Otherwise, go at it in much the same way. The horizontal lines are drawn 2" apart and the *very light* vertical lines are drawn 1³⁄₁₆" apart. (See Figure 3-16C.)

---

*The first time I worked on this larger model I made the mistake of approaching this problem mathematically by laying out a series of equilateral triangles that were drawn with tolerances so high they squeaked. All my pride in my mathematical finesse was soon dashed when I discovered to my chagrin that no matter how beautiful these tolerances looked on paper, in paper *folding* I had made no accommodation for the topological demands of the *thickness* of the paper! What initially appeared to be mathematically perfect was soon demonstrated to be a practical failure.

Moral: sometimes the less tolerance you insist upon the more tolerant you become!

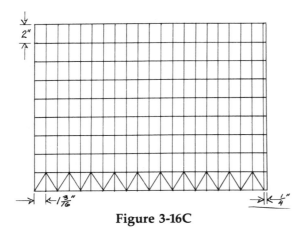

Figure 3-16C

ASSEMBLING, DECORATING AND OPERATING INSTRUCTIONS

YOU NEED:

preruled and precut flexagon strips
rulers or short Straight-Edges*
pencils with sharp points
paste, scissors, and crayons

ASSEMBLING INSTRUCTIONS

1. Once the long flexagon strips have been cut on the horizontal dividing lines, have your kids use their pencils and rulers (or Straight-Edges) to draw a series of equilateral triangles shown here in Figure 3-16D. Those end areas indicated by shading are then cut away. The remaining strip

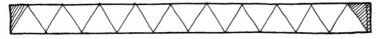

Figure 3-16D

*See Glossary.

is folded carefully on the lines and then refolded so that the folds will be encouraged to lose their directional "memory."

2. Have your kids lay their strips in front of them so that the longest edge is toward them as shown in Figure 3-16E. Loop one end over the other as shown in Figure 3-16F and pencil in a "P" (for "paste") in each of the exposed end triangles as shown.

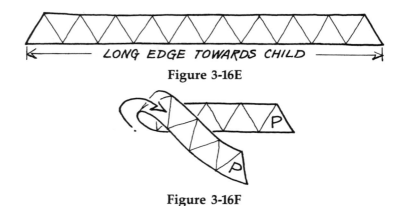

Figure 3-16E

Figure 3-16F

3. Now from this point on until the flexagon is ready for pasting, you will have to Quarterback* this activity. The following folding operation is therefore *your* job. (While this operation looks long and complicated, it is really very simple, and moves along quite rapidly.)

> *One:* Turn the strip on its back, and rotate the right-hand end upward to "10 o'clock" position, as shown in Figure 3-16G.

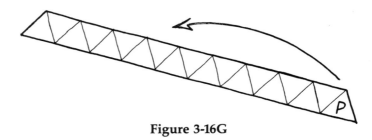

Figure 3-16G

---

*See Glossary.

Two: Fold the top over as shown in Figure 3-16H.

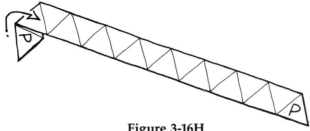

Figure 3-16H

Three: Continue this wrap-around, over and under, folding operation (see Figure 3-16I) until you arrive at
the "check point" position indicated in Figure
3-16J.

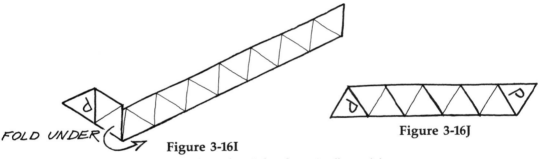

Figure 3-16J

Figure 3-16I

4. Once you have arrived at the "check point" position
where both pasting tabs are up, carefully flip this whole
subassembly over on its belly into the position indicated in
Figure 3-16K.

Figure 3-16K

5. Now for the big finish:

One: Fold the left-hand side of this strip under the
right as shown in Figure 3-16L.

Figure 3-16L

Two: Fold the bottom of the tail *under* the top of the tail and *over* the top of this nearly completed flexagon as shown in Figure 3-16M.

Figure 3-16M

Three: Flip this flexagon over and instruct the proud owner to "paste the two P's together." (See Figures 3-16N and 3-16O.)

Figure 3-16N   Figure 3-16O

DECORATING INSTRUCTIONS

The reason that the flexagon is so highly entertaining lies not only in the surprising ways in which the various faces disappear and reappear but also in the amusing way in which the six triangles that compose each face mysteriously alter and re-alter their design in a kaleidoscopic fashion. For obvious reasons your kids should be instructed to keep their designs not only simple but directional, for a design that is needlessly complex or that is lacking in direction does not show its best face when "sent through" this hexagonal shuffling machine. Figures 3-16P, 3-16Q, and 3-16R graph-

Figure 3-16P   Figure 3-16Q   Figure 3-16R

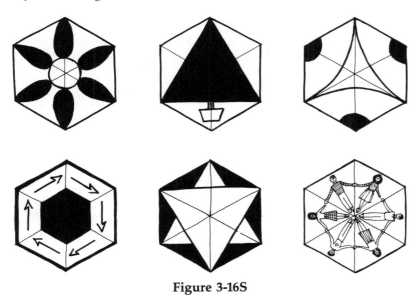

Figure 3-16S

ically illustrate the kinds of transformation that can take place with a single design. See Figure 3-16S for additional suggestions.

FLEXING INSTRUCTIONS

As stated earlier, this lesson is best Quarterbacked* for once it gets underway no two children will ever be on the same procedural step. Here is how I proceed from here:

Once your kids understand how to go about decorating both sides of their flexagons, it won't be long before some of the speedier members return with a "completed" flexagon and a what-now? look on their faces. What I do at this point is this: I take the "finished" flexagon, secretly flexing it while I pretend to examine it (see flexing instructions below), and then with mock disapproval written all over my face, I say, "I thought I told you to decorate *both* sides of this hexagon."

Since each flexing performs two tricks: it makes one side vanish and rearranges the other, the room will soon begin to hum with extraordinary excitement.

---

*See Glossary.

While in the beginning it is a lot more fun to continue your secret flexing and mock disapproval routine, it won't be long before they all catch on to the operating instructions, which are as follows:

1.   Grasp two adjoining triangles of your flexagon with your thumb and forefinger as shown in Figure 3-16T.

2.   Press in the opposite side of the flexagon as shown in Figures 3-16U and 3-16V. Place your thumb into the center of this budding "hexaflower" and open it up to expose the hidden surface.

Figure 3-16T

Figure 3-16U

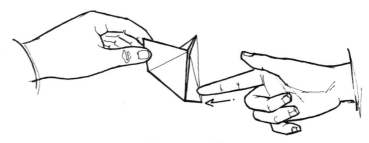

Figure 3-16V

ADDITIONAL SUGGESTIONS

As any veteran hexaflexer will tell you, the most efficient way to go about exposing all faces of this entertaining device is to continue to flex from the same flexing point until it refuses to flex any further. Then move to the neighboring flexing position and continue to flex as before. While there is no point in telling your kids the total number of faces (for this would destroy much of the fun and gain nothing in return), it might be helpful for *you* to know that there are six completely different faces to be found and that each of these six faces can reappear in two or three different kaleidoscopic transformations!

Again, do not let the length of this lesson or its seemingly complex instructions dissuade you from attempting it. Like many other processes, the making of a flexagon is easier to do than to talk about, and once mastered it is *yours* forever!

GLOSSARY

BACK - RUBBING

When certain kinds of drawings are belly-flopped onto another piece of paper and given a vigorous back rub with a hard, smooth object, a certain amount of image transference takes place. For obvious reasons I call this process *Back-Rubbing*.

As you might suppose, Back-Rubbing is impossible without a *Back-Rubber*. In a classroom setting I find it convenient to have my kids use metal scissor handles as Back-Rubbers (See Figure G-1), but many other objects will work just as well (including the end of a ruler or even a thumb nail!).

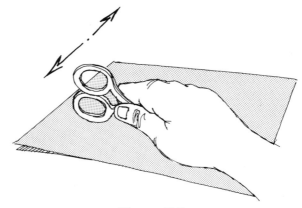

Figure G-1

CIRCLECONES

For all practical purposes spherical or hemispherical shapes are impossible to construct from paper. For a classroom substitute for a hemisphere, *Circlecones* do just fine. Here is how to make them:

1. Cut out a circle and draw a line from the center to the perimeter as shown in Figure G-2. Cut on this line.
2. Overlap A over B and paste. Your Circlecone is now complete! (See Figure G-3.)

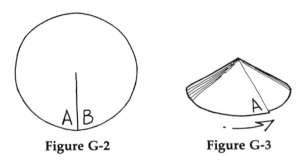

Figure G-2   **Figure G-3**

MEASURING STRIPS

If for some idiotic reason or other it was suddenly decreed that *only* those who could demonstrate competence with a ruler could remain in school, teachers would suddenly find themselves sitting in empty—or nearly empty—classrooms. The truth is that very few kids can make efficient use of a ruler. Some have trouble just manipulating it, others have trouble reading the calibrations, all have trouble using it to *accurately* draw such things as vertical and horizontal lines. *That's* why I employ *Measuring Strips*.

A Measuring Strip is a piece of paperboard cut to a premeasured width. For example, let us say that you have a 9" square of construction paper that you would like your kids to divide into nine 3" squares. You can spend the rest of the day teaching these kids how to use a ruler* or you can pass out 3″ × 9″ Measuring Strips, and show your kids how to use these simple tools as demonstrated in Figures G-4 and G-5.

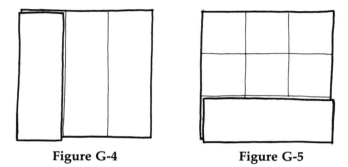

Figure G-4 **Figure G-5**

PAPER FOLDING INSTRUCTIONS

Who would ever have predicted that you would some day find yourself flipping through a glossary looking for instructions on how to fold a piece of paper? What's to know?

You may know how to fold paper properly for an art activity, but—unless *you* tell *them*—kids don't. Unless the instructions read otherwise, the best procedure is always to *unfold* each fold before proceeding to the next. Figures G-6 through G-13 should explain everything. The untutored method, in which the folds are not unfolded before making additional folds, results in lumpy packets that when unfolded look something like that pictured in Figure G-14.

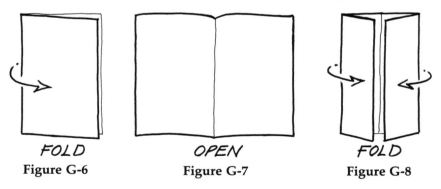

FOLD *OPEN* *FOLD*

Figure G-6 **Figure G-7** **Figure G-8**

---

*I suggest that you save all ruler instructions for math periods, for if there is anything that can bog down an art activity, it is a joyless interruption of this kind!

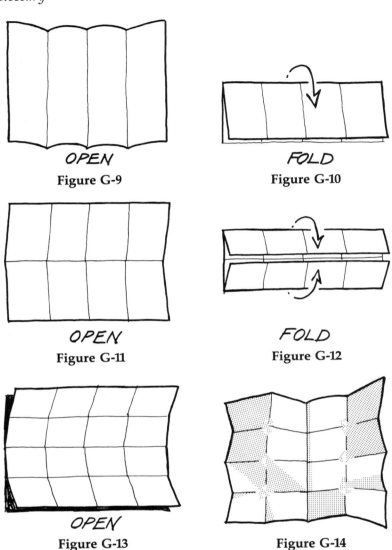

OPEN
Figure G-9

FOLD
Figure G-10

OPEN
Figure G-11

FOLD
Figure G-12

OPEN
Figure G-13

Figure G-14

PAPER-POKER

There are times when the center of a piece of paper or paperboard needs to be removed. If the material is paper, any sharp object will make the initial puncture so that the scissors can be used to finish the job. In this case a pencil point or the point of a scissor blade is all that's needed and this is generally a task that most children can do for themselves.

On the other hand, if the material is paperboard, your kids are going to need help. I carry a Swiss Army Knife that has a tool that answers my needs. You'll have to find your own!

Either way, once the puncture has been made, the kids can then stick one blade of their scissors into the hole and proceed to finish the job.

PINCH-FOLD

A Pinch-Fold is not really a fold at all, it is a near-fold, a short crease normally used to determine the halfway point on one or more edges of a sheet of (otherwise) unfolded paper. See Figures G-15 and G-16.

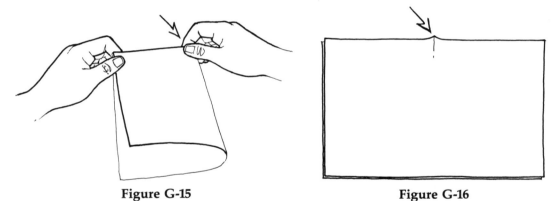

Figure G-15   **Figure G-16**

QUARTERBACKING

Some activities are best directed from the front of the classroom; others function best when counseled in small groups. I call this counseling huddle *Quarterbacking*.

SAILBOAT FOLD, SAILBOAT CONE, ETC.

SAILBOAT FOLD: The fold demonstrated in Figure G-17.

SAILBOAT CONE: Instructions for Making

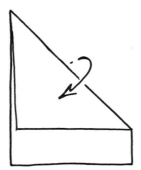

Figure G-17

1. Fold a sheet of rectangular paper according to the above instructions.
2. Fold up the "boat" to overlap the "sail" and paste as shown in Figure G-18.
3. Turn this folded paper over to paste down the remaining flap. (See Figure G-19.)
4. That's it—if it opens up like a duncecap, you've done it! (See Figure G-20.)

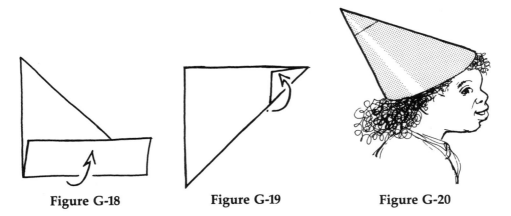

Figure G-18 **Figure G-19** **Figure G-20**

PERFECT SAILBOAT CONE: Once you have made a *Sailboat Cone,* use point A as a center to swing arc B-C. Cut on B-C and you have constructed a *Perfect Sailboat Cone!* (See Figure G-21.)

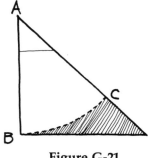

Figure G-21

SCRIBBLE-CANCELING

To clearly identify those sections of a cut-paper project what are to be cut away, or to identify the "wrong side" of a sheet of paper, I find it efficiently convenient to simply instruct my kids to scribble on those parts that are to be so identified.

STRAIGHT-EDGES

Rulers are handy for a lot of things. They make good paste dispensers, they make a resounding attention-getting *whack* when struck against the top of a desk, and they can sometimes be used as Back-Rubbers (see page 208). But since very few kids know how to use them for measuring, I find very little use for them in an art class. For one thing I never seem to have enough on hand, and those that I do are often so badly battered as to be nearly worthless. My answer to all of this is simply to cut up strips of scrap paperboard whenever the need arises. These paperboard strips have a lot to commend them: they are straight, they are inferior classroom weapons, and they don't bear all those strange calibrations that so thoroughly confuse my kids. They are also cheap and expendable. I call these things *Straight-Edges*.

INDEX